J. D. Edgar

Canada and its capital

With sketches of political and social life at Ottawa

J. D. Edgar

Canada and its capital
With sketches of political and social life at Ottawa

ISBN/EAN: 9783742876324

Manufactured in Europe, USA, Canada, Australia, Japa

Cover: Foto ©Andreas Hilbeck / pixelio.de

Manufactured and distributed by brebook publishing software (www.brebook.com)

J. D. Edgar

Canada and its capital

WITH

SKETCHES OF POLITICAL AND SOCIAL LIFE
AT OTTAWA

BY

HON. J. D. EDGAR,
Q.C., M.P., F.R.S.C.

THE SPEAKER, COMMONS OF CANADA

TORONTO:
GEORGE N. MORANG
1898.

PREFACE.

With the material growth of Canada, and her expansion into a nation, there has arisen among her citizens a natural pride in her political institutions. The Canadian political capital has become a place of interest. But the distances which separate different parts of the Dominion from one another, and the fact that Ottawa lies somewhat off the main route of travel, have prevented many Canadians from visiting the seat of Government. There is much that they would like to know about Ottawa, and the doings of the people there. One object of the following chapters is to give the needed information. The impressions formed of the Canadian Capital by a transient English writer might have the merit of impartiality, but they would not be based upon a full experience. One whose political duties have, for a lengthened period, annually taken him

PREFACE.

to Ottawa, from another part of Canada, is likely to possess some of the fairness of an outsider, and sufficient experience to enable him to pourtray the Canadian Capital and its political and social life.

The many strangers who visit Ottawa, from time to time, are warm in praise of its beauties, and are attracted by its system of government. Some of them are curious to know about its public men, its social life, its summer and winter sports, and even its literature. It is believed that this little volume will interest that class of travellers, and also a considerable portion of the reading public outside of Canada, whose attention has, during the Jubilee year, been so much aroused regarding the Dominion and its people.

OTTAWA, March, 1898.

CONTENTS

CHAPTER I.
The Site of the Capital 1

CHAPTER II.
The Ottawa Under the French Régime 11

CHAPTER III.
A Legend of the Ottawa 26

CHAPTER IV.
The Story of Philemon Wright 35

CHAPTER V.
How Ottawa Came to be the Capital of Canada 49

CHAPTER VI.
The National Buildings 53

CHAPTER VII.
The Canadian System of Government 68

CHAPTER VIII.
The House of Commons 83

CHAPTER IX.

Three Canadian Statesmen. Pen Sketches of Laurier, Tupper and Cartwright 97

CHAPTER X.

Vice-Regal Functions 112

CHAPTER XI.

Winter Sports at Ottawa 121

CHAPTER XII.

Ottawa Summer Sports 134

CHAPTER XIII.

Literature of the Capital 153

CHAPTER XIV.

Some Ottawa Poets 158

CHAPTER XV.

An Epitome of Leading Events from 1861 to 1898   179

CHAPTER XVI.

The Future of Canada 190

CHAPTER XVII.

Canada and England 200

List of Illustrations

Hon. J. D. Edgar, Speaker, Commons of Canada	Frontispiece
Rideau Falls	5
Chaudière Falls .. .. -	6
National Buildings	53
Parliament Buildings and Library, from the west ..	55
Western Departmental Block and Mackenzie Tower	57
Eastern Departmental Block	64
Hon. C. A. P. Pelletier, Speaker, Senate of Canada .	70
Southern Departmental Block	74
Commons Chamber	83
Rt. Hon. Sir Wilfrid Laurier	99
Sir Charles Tupper	104
Sir Richard Cartwright	108
The Earl of Aberdeen	112
Senate Chamber	114
Government House	117
Vice-Regal Curling	128
Tobogganing	130
Lovers' Walk	135
Library of Parliament	158
Houses of Parliament—front view..	179

CHAPTER I.

THE SITE OF THE CAPITAL.

The Choice of National Capitals——Ottawa's Site and Buildings ——Canadians proud of Them——View from the Terrace——Laurentian Range——The Tawny Ottawa——The Gatineau River——Curtain Falls——The Rideau——Great Chaudière Falls——Champlain's Description of Them——The Devil's Hole——Indians believed it Haunted ——City of Hull across the River, in the Province of Quebec——Sawmills and Factories——Col. By and the Rideau Canal——An Imperial Work——Its Object——Bytown——Major's Hill Park.

National capitals are seldom the result of deliberate choice. They, for the most part, grow with the race, as in the case of Rome, Paris, or London. Yet some which have been chosen in the wilderness have more than justified the boldness of their founders. Alexandria waxed great and rich on the banks of the Nile; so did St. Petersburg on the Neva; and Washington on the Potomac bids fair to excel them both in stately splendour. All these cities took the names of their founders, but when Queen Victoria, in 1858, chose, upon the banks of the Ottawa, the place for Canada's capital, she left it with the picturesque name of that beautiful river.

When a country is young, and its history is not yet told in monuments nor typified in ancient architecture, its capital should be adorned in other ways. The Tower of London and the memories that cluster round Westminster Hall must help to inspire even prosaic members of the British Parliament with a dominant consciousness of the continuity of the government in which they are taking part, and of the enduring nature of the laws they are helping to frame. Wise, then, were the advisers of the Queen, when, to compensate for the absence of monuments of the past, they gave to Canada for her capital, a site of surpassing beauty; and equally to be commended were those who conceived and carried out the glorious national buildings with which the rocky heights of Ottawa are crowned.

It cannot be denied that the patriotism of the Athenian was kindled at the sight of the Acropolis, and that every Scottish heart beats high when he sees the ancient castle on Edin's Hill. To fill a Canadian with pride in his country, and confidence in its future, shew him the noble pile of the national buildings as they tower and glitter in the setting sun, far above the foaming river. It may not be a logical ground for his patriotism, but it is a sentimental one, and it will influence his feelings and his actions when he goes back to his distant home, whether it be on the western prairie, on the shores of the Atlantic, or on the far-off Pacific Slope.

Standing on the Terrace behind the Parliament buildings, and looking to the north across the river, the view is only bounded by the wooded Chelsea Hills, a branch of the great Laurentian Range, which uplifts its shaggy heights for hundreds of miles, away down to the Gulf of St. Lawrence. A gap is distinctly visible among the hills, where the River Gatineau flings its wild torrent, in its southerly course, to join the Ottawa. Raging rapids and fierce falls roar and echo among those trees and rocks. Placid lakes lie embosomed in the hills, and pour their overflow of crystal waters through wooded glens and down foaming cataracts, to reach peace again in the valleys far below. In spring, those woods are carpeted with a garden of brilliant-hued wild flowers—painted and snow-white trilliums, lilies of the valley, trailing arbutus, wood daffodils, anemones, hepaticas, violets of every hue, moccasin flowers and other orchids, and blossoms without number. In the autumn, the brilliant tints of the leaves of the deciduous trees, mingling with strips of dark-hued pines, or spruce, along the sides of the hills and in the valleys, make a gorgeous picture; and bold would be the artist who would attempt to paint it in all its truth and glory of colour.

RIDEAU FALLS AT OTTAWA, IN WINTER.

TWO BEAUTIFUL RIVERS.

In the foreground, and close under the wooded cliff, flows the tawny Ottawa, still flecked with the foam of its cataract. Though only an affluent of the St. Lawrence, it is still so vast a stream as to be best comparable in volume with the Danube among the rivers of Europe. A couple of miles below it receives the waters of the Gatineau, drawn from the northern forests for a distance of more than three hundred miles. A smaller stream flows from the south and plunges headlong in double, curtain-like falls, over a rocky ledge into the Ottawa, only a mile east of the buildings, and within the city limits. The earliest French *voyageurs* passing up the Grand River (as the Ottawa was for them), seeing this "slow-dropping veil of thinnest lawn," exclaimed, "*Le Rideau! Le Rideau!*" Thus was a name found, not only for the river and its falls, but for the streets and clubs, rifle ranges and canals of the capital, and for Government House itself, which is locally known as Rideau Hall.

What is that sonorous diapason of sound that is wafted down the river on the western breeze and attracts the eye to a seething, tumbling mass of white foam about a mile away? It is the eternal voice of the Great Chaudière, where the waters of the Grand River burst with resistless power through a narrow chasm of rock to boil and smoke in the "big cauldron below." Nearly three hundred years ago, Champlain thus described the scene:—

"The water falls at one point with such impetuosity upon the rock that it has, in the course of time, worn out a wide and deep basin. Into this the water rushes with a whirling motion, boiling up tumultuously in the midst, so that the Indians call it *Asticou*, which means 'cauldron,' (*Chaudière*). This waterfall produces a noise that may be heard two leagues away."

Above the Chaudière, for a couple of miles, the river is very wide, and is broken with rapids and studded with islands so that, seen from Parliament Hill in the sunlight, it has the effect of a sparkling lake. A few hundred feet east of the Great Chaudière, a

ments of rock and debris thrown in from the blasting out of artificial channels. Yet any passer-by can still look down from the roadway on the Hull side of the bridge, and see the waters foaming far below in the mysterious depths where the Indians believed an evil spirit dwelt.

The Ottawa river is the boundary between the provinces of Quebec and Ontario, and a fine suspension bridge connects the English with the French province, a hundred yards below the Chaudière Falls. The Dominion capital is at one end of the bridge, and at the other is the busy manufacturing city of Hull, with a population now largely French. The utilitarian spirit of the age has altered the smiling face of nature nowhere more than at the Chaudière. That inexhaustible source of power has created a great milling and manufacturing centre. Its surplus waters drive some of the largest sawmills in the world, whose raw material of white pine logs is floated down to them on the same friendly waters for hundreds of miles. Flour mills, pulp mills, match factories, electric works, and industries of all kinds crowd every foot of available space below the Falls, whose conserved energy turns wheels which furnish employment to an army of men, and feed nearly fifteen thousand hungry mouths.

Up to 1826, a wild, rocky gorge cleft the hill immediately to the east of the present site of the buildings. It was in that year seized upon by Col. By, of the Royal Engineers, as the northern outlet of an important military work, the Rideau Canal. At the close of the war with the United States, of 1812-14, the British Government felt the strategic weakness of leaving the Province of Upper Canada connected with Montreal and Quebec only by the frontier route along the St. Lawrence. They accordingly decided to make a canal from the fortified harbor of Kingston, on Lake Ontario, to the River Ottawa which enters the St. Lawrence near Montreal. The River Rideau and the lakes on its course supplied part of the water for the canal, and the gorge referred to offered a natural passage through which the drop could be made, by means of a system of locks, to the Ottawa from the upper levels.

A settlement of some importance had already been made at Hull across the river, but only a few houses had been built in the woods on the Upper Canada side, when Col. By took up his residence there to construct the extensive locks required. The hamlet grew to a village and the village to a town, both gratefully accepting the unmusical name of "Bytown," which was borne until 1854, when Bytown became the city of Ottawa.

Looking across the canal locks, and on a slightly lower level than Parliament Hill, we see the beautiful little park of Major's Hill, and beyond that Nepean Point, a rocky promontory overlooking the river, and adding much to the rugged beauty of the scene.

CHAPTER II.

THE OTTAWA UNDER THE FRENCH REGIME.

The French Explorers——The River of the Algonquins or the Grand River——Champlain passes up the Ottawa, 1613——The Traitor De Vignan and the North Sea——Start from St. Helen's Island——Arrival below the Chaudière——What met the Eye of the Founder, of Quebec——Portage at the Falls——He goes no further than Alumette Island——Dramatic Exposure of De Vignan, the Impostor, by the Indian Chief——Champlain returns——Mystic Rites performed by Indians at the Chaudière——Ambush of the Iroquois——The Canoe Route from New York——Champlain again passed up the Ottawa, 1615——Le Caron——Both returned, 1616——Passage up of Jesuits, 1626——Breboeuf's Dreams and Visions——His Mission Among the Hurons——His Martyrdom in 1649——Dispersion of the Hurons——Their Last Passage Down the Ottawa——Story of a Visit by LaSalle——Sulpicians make the Passage——Iroquois Blockade the River in Spite of Frontenac——Pontiac, a Chief of the Ottawas——Led them at Braddock's Defeat——Passage by English Traders——Massacre at Mackinaw.

The political history of Ottawa began less than forty years ago, with the events which led to its becoming the Canadian capital, but we have glimpses of an older time in the thrilling narrative of Champlain and the precious records of the Jesuit missionaries. To the earliest French explorers, the Ottawa was known as "*la riviere des Algoumequins,*" the river of the Algonquins. The Algonquin race included many tribes, one of which, the Ottawas, dwelt upon the banks of the river and finally gave it their name.

Samuel de Champlain, the illustrious founder of Quebec, the brave soldier and sailor, the daring explorer, and the observant writer, in his story of his fourth voyage of discovery, gives a description of his first trip up the Ottawa, made in 1613.

Champlain had sent a young Frenchman, Nicolas de Vignan by name, up the Ottawa, with friendly Indians, two years before, and his traveller had returned with the marvellous story that he had reached the North Sea. He related that the Ottawa River had its rise in a lake which also discharged itself into the sea, and that the journey could be made in a few days. He also gave a most circumstantial account of having seen the wreck of an English ship. The honest navigator was completely taken in, and lost no time in starting off to verify a discovery which the world was hoping for, with feverish anxiety. His fleet consisted of two canoes with one Indian (afterwards he secured a second) and three Frenchmen, one of them being DeVignan. They left St. Helen's Island, at present in Montreal Harbour, on Monday the 27th of May, and pushed on up rapids, wherever a canoe could pass, and by land portages where the current was too strong, until on the night of the 3rd of June, they camped a few miles below the Chaudière. On the morning of Tuesday, 4th June, 1613, two frail and battered canoes were launched on the broad bosom of the unknown river. In one was the traitor De Vignan, in the other glanced the fearless, honest eyes of his dupe, wide with wonder at the sights he saw. The time of year was just when the waters of the North were brought down from the melting of the snows, and the streams were at their fullest. On his right, Champlain sees the surging flood of the Gatineau coming to swell the Ottawa, whose brimming waters gleam among the trees on the river's edge. He is told by his Indian guide that his tribe often seek the fastnesses of the Upper Gatineau to hide from the dreaded Iroquois. Soon he is lost in admiration of the twin curtain falls of the Rideau on his left hand, and his guide tells him that the waters form an arcade under which the Indians delight to walk, and where they are only wet by the spray. He sees beyond those fair curtain falls, cliff rising above cliff, each sheer from the river, clothed with clinging vines or gleaming birch, and crowned in majesty with mighty monarchs of the forest. The sky is clear, but the air is filled with a strange thunder. As they round a lofty headland, he sees a cloud of mist, and soon is able to distinguish beneath it the mad violence of waters that had for ages been making their solemn music, heard only by the red savage and by the wild birds and beasts of the wilderness.

Five years before this, Champlain's unerring eye had chosen the rock of Quebec for the capital of New France. Did no inspiration tell him that he now beheld the heights on which would stand the capital, not only of the New France that he was winning for his king, but of vast territories stretching to the unknown western sea?

The rapid current did not give him long to dream or to admire, but he tells us that they paddled up as near as possible to the Falls, "where the Indians took the canoes, and our Frenchmen and myself our arms, provisions, and other commodities." He describes with great feeling the sharp and rugged rocks of the portages to pass the falls and the rapids, until at last, in the afternoon, they embarked upon the peaceful waters of a lake, "where there were very beautiful islands filled with vines, walnut and other agreeable trees." The butternut was evidently mistaken for the walnut, which it so closely resembles.

This journey of Champlain came to an abrupt close a few days afterwards, when he reached Allumette Island some seventy miles up the river. Here was a large settlement of friendly Algonquins, called "*les sauvages de l'Ile*," and the traveller sought to obtain from them several canoes and guides to proceed further. They had their own commercial reasons for keeping the French apart from other tribes, for fear of their own traffic as intermediaries being injured. They dwelt upon the difficulties of the trip, and especial warnings were given of the supernatural dangers of meeting the terrible tribe of Sorcerers who dwelt at Lake Nipissing. Champlain explained that his young man, De Vignan, had passed through all these dangers. Then every eye was fixed upon the impostor, and the head chief addressed him: "Is it true that you have said that you had been among the Sorcerers?" After a long pause he answered, "Yes, I have been there." The Indians at once threw themselves upon him, with fierce cries, as if they would have eaten him, or torn him in pieces, and the chief said, "You are a bold liar! You well know that every night you slept by my side with my children. How have you the impudence to tell your chief such lies, and the wickedness to expose his life among such dangers?" The upshot of the disclosures was the disgrace of De Vignan, and the speedy return of Champlain down the Ottawa with an escort of fifty canoes. About the 15th of June, the party reached the falls of the Chaudière, where the savages performed their customary mystic rites, which Champlain describes in these words: "After having carried their canoes to the foot of the falls, they gather in a certain spot, where one of them, provided with a wooden dish, passed it round, and each one places in the dish a piece of tobacco.

The collection finished, the dish is placed in the midst of the band, and all dance around it, chanting after their fashion. Then one of the chiefs delivers a harangue, explaining that from olden times they have always made such an offering, and that by this means they are protected from their enemies and saved from misfortune—for so the devil persuades them; and they live in this and many other superstitions. Then the same chief takes up the dish and proceeds to throw the tobacco into the Chaudière, amid the loud shoutings of the band. These poor people are so superstitious that they do not believe they can make a safe journey if they have not performed this ceremony at this particular place, the more so because their enemies often lie in wait for them, and surprise them at this portage, not venturing further on account of the dangers of the route."

What picture can be more striking, of the scenes that have been enacted time and again, for centuries past, at the Chaudière Falls?

The exorcising of the demons of the place by mystic pagan rites, the silent ambush, the fierce slaughter by the sudden foe! The rich imagination of Fenimore Cooper never clothed a spot with associations more weird and thrilling than Champlain's simple narrative has thrown around the very soil of the Canadian capital.

When it is remembered that the highways for the journeys of the savages were the rivers and lakes, and that for transport wagons they had only bark canoes, it can be understood why the Iroquois were so frequently found at the Chaudière Falls of the Ottawa. From their home in the northern part of New York State, they crossed the upper St. Lawrence to Kingston. At that point began the remarkable system of waterways, lakes, and rivers, which afforded a perfect canoe route to the Chaudière, and which has since been converted into a steamboat route by the engineers of the Rideau Canal. The tribes of the interior, in their trips either up or down the river, were forced at this place to leave the water and make a tedious portage through the forest, to pass the falls and rapids. Struggling through woods and rocks, loaded with canoes and bales of fur, they became an easy prey to the Iroquois lying in ambush there.

The indomitable Champlain again ascended the Ottawa, in 1615, and went through by Lake Nipissing and French River to the Georgian Bay, and south to the Huron settlements. No adventures marked his journey up the Grand River, but it is recorded that he fraternized with the dreaded Sorcerers of Lake Nipissing. He had been preceded by one week in this journey by the Recollet priest, LeCaron, who was the first Christian missionary to explore the route that led to the Huron missions in the northeastern part of the County of Simcoe, and the first white man to visit that tribe in their homes. Both the missionary and the soldier returning, passed again under the Ottawa cliffs in 1616, but while one had been spreading Christianity among the Hurons, the other had been leading them to battle against their Iroquois foes.

The Falls of the Chaudière were not seen again by a white man until 1626, when three Jesuit fathers whom Champlain had brought from France the year before, passed up on their way to found their Huron mission, so famous and so tragic. Their leader was Jean de Breboeuf, a noble of Normandie, and a heroic soldier of the cross. He had heard from Champlain of the beauties of the demon-haunted Chaudière, of the curtain-falls and the shaggy cliffs. He saw visions and dreamed dreams among the Hurons. Did he foresee, in dream or vision, when he slept within sound of those wild waters, the churches that would one day raise their stately spires on both sides of the river, and ring out their clanging bells above the noise of those pagan falls of Asticou?

Everyone knows the fate of Breboeuf.

How he dwelt with the Hurons and was their friend, their teacher, their general, until the fatal day, the 16th of March, 1649, when the savage Iroquois burst with fierce yells upon the peaceful village of St. Louis. Breboeuf and Lalemant, another priest, were cruelly tortured to death. Breboeuf's remains were recovered, and his skull is to-day enshrined as a sacred relic in the Hotel Dieu at Quebec.

While the Jesuit missions existed among the Hurons, the Ottawa river was filled with fleets of canoes, manned by the Indian fur hunters from the Huron and Algonquin tribes, on their way to trade at Quebec, and at the newer post of Ville Marie (Montreal). Soon after Breboeuf's death, the whole Huron nation was scattered or destroyed by the Iroquois. The next year, the Jesuits abandoned the mission and led a remnant of about three hundred Hurons, by the familiar Ottawa route, to Quebec. They found that the Iroquois wolves had slain or scattered all the tribes of the river. The Sorcerers of the

Lake had disappeared. The Nation of the Isle had deserted their peaceful homes on Allumette Island. One wonders if the fugitive Hurons were permitted by the priests, when passing the Chaudière Falls, to practise their accustomed pagan rites for appeasing the evil spirit of the Devil's Hole. We may be sure that when they had passed the falls, all the travellers saw the frowning cliffs and the distant hills, for the last time, without regret, and without hope of any future for that romantic piece of wilderness.

There is a curious story told by the famous French explorer, Perrot, that he met LaSalle, the great discoverer of the Mississippi, in the summer of 1670, hunting with a party of Iroquois on the Ottawa. This was during the two years of LaSalle's career, when his biographers cannot fully account for his movements. At any rate, it is recorded that in the same summer, two Sulpician priests had made their way from Lake Huron, down the Ottawa route to Quebec, and it is probable that upper lake tribes took the risk every year of Iroquois ambuscades, and made the same trip for purposes of trade. Twenty years later, the Iroquois formed a great war camp at the mouth of the Ottawa, and ravaged all the French settlements within reach. Even the strong arm of Frontenac could not keep the foe in check. Parkman well describes the position: "The River Ottawa was the main artery of Canada, and to stop it was to stop the flow of her life-blood. The Iroquois knew this, and their constant effort was to close it so completely that the annual supply of beaver skins would be prevented from passing, and the colony be compelled to live on credit. It was their habit to spend the latter part of the winter in hunting among the forests between the Ottawa and the upper St. Lawrence, and then, when the ice broke up, to move in large bands to the banks of the former stream, and lie in ambush at the Chaudière, the Long Sault, or other favorable points, to waylay the passing canoes. On the other hand, it was the constant effort of Frontenac to drive them off, and keep the river open—an almost impossible task."

The Algonquin tribes of the Ottawa were scattered like the Ten Tribes of Israel. The one which gave its name to the river became a power on the shores of the upper lakes, and under its great chief, Pontiac, took part in the defeat of Braddock at the battle of Monongahela, in 1755.

After the conquest of Canada, the English traders lost no time in competing for the fur trade of the Ottawa, and we read of some of their number passing up that stream in 1763. In the same year the English survivors of the treacherous massacre at Fort Michillimackinac, (Mackinaw), passed under the Ottawa cliffs, on their way to Montreal.

CHAPTER III.

A LEGEND OF THE OTTAWA.—THE DEATH SONG OF CADIEUX.

Legends of Iroquois' Massacres—Falls of the Grand Calumet—The Grave of Cadieux—His Story—Wedded to an Algonquin—A Trading Party—"The Iroquois!"—A Strategem to save the Women and Children—Their Safety secured—Bravery of Cadieux—His Wanderings—His Camp—Alarm of Iroquois—Prove to be French—He faints from Excitement—Left alone Again—His Body found—His "Lament"—A Popular and Touching French Canadian Song.

About seventy miles up the river from the capital, lies a spot which is still haunted by legends of the days when the fierce Iroquois swept down upon the peaceful traders of the Algonquin tribes, ruthlessly robbing, torturing and massacring their victims. Here, in the falls of the Grand Calumet, the river plunges in three separate streams over jagged granite cliffs, some sixty feet in height, and then rushes foaming onward in a succession of smaller cascades, called the Seven Falls. It whirls in swift eddies round points of black rock, and rises in white spray as it dashes angrily against the rude boulders that strive in vain to impede its tumultuous downward rush.

On the portage, which leads past this dangerous portion of the river, and just at the foot of the Island of the Grand Calumet, a mouldering wooden cross marks a lonely grave. Here lies the body of the *voyageur* Cadieux, and the tale that is told of his death is a strange and pathetic one.

Cadieux was a French *voyageur* who had acquired some slight education before leaving the old world, and who had, moreover, some natural talent for music and verse. He wedded an Algonquin maiden, and frequently joined parties of that tribe in their hunting expeditions, returning with them to Montreal, and acting as interpreter between them and his own countrymen. One spring he, with a few other families, had camped on the portage of the Seven Falls, just below the Grand Fall of the Calumet. They were awaiting a band of friendly Indians with whom they might travel to Montreal, there to dispose of their furs. All was peace in the camp, when suddenly a young Indian, who had been roaming in the woods below the portage, rushed in with the dreaded cry, "The Iroquois! The Iroquois!" There was no time to be lost. Escape into the woods was impossible, encumbered as they were by their women and children. Their only hope was to shoot the rapids, hitherto considered impassable. But even if their frail barks carried them safely through the angry, seething waters, the Iroquois, finding traces of their recent camp, would pursue them and overtake them before they could reach a place of safety. In order to prevent this, some of the party would have to remain behind, and delay the enemy at the portage. Cadieux, with one young brave, undertook this dangerous task. They set forth well armed, and placed themselves in ambush in the middle of the portage. Their first shot was to be the sign that all the Iroquois had left the river, and that the fugitives would, therefore, be out of their sight. Within an hour the expected signal was heard, and the frail canoes shot into the midst of the raging waters. Tossed here and there, with sharp rocks eager to crush them on every side, the paddlers, both men and women, strained every nerve to avoid the boulders and guide their frail canoes into the deeper currents. Before leaving, they had invoked the aid of Ste. Anne, and the story goes that a tall, white lady hovered ever before them, and showed them their course until they safely gained the calm waters below.

In the meantime, Cadieux and his companion, well hidden in the woods, at some distance apart, had engaged the attention of the Iroquois. Firing rapidly from different directions, they had killed several of the enemy, and the suddenness of the attack had produced a slight panic. The Iroquois, thinking that a large party was attacking them, hesitated, and in the confusion, Cadieux and his companion retired further into the wood. In a moment the hostile party was pursuing them, and before long the young Algonquin brave was killed. Cadieux escaped, but for days he wandered about, faint with hunger, and worn out by constant watching and by anxiety concerning the fate of his friends. At length, he heard the roar of the rapids, and hoping to find himself far down the river and out of reach of the pursuers, he eagerly hastened in the direction of the sound. Alas! after days of wandering, he had but moved in a circle, and was again on the spot where he had parted from his companions. His ammunition had been exhausted and starvation seemed imminent. Too ill and weary to set forth again on his journey, he built a shelter of boughs, and lived for a time on whatever food he could find close by. Returning one day from a short foraging expedition, he saw the smoke of a camp-fire rising through the trees near his hut. Thinking a party of Iroquois were in possession of it, he remained in concealment. Suddenly three figures appeared, and, to his amazement, he saw that they were Frenchmen of his own party, who had evidently returned in search of him. The shock was too great for his feeble frame; he sank on his knees incapable of movement; his lips refused to utter the cry which would bring them to him, and they passed out of his sight.

Some days later they returned, and there, a few feet from the little hut, they saw a wooden cross. It stood at the head of an open grave, in which, half covered by green branches lay the body of their friend. Feeling his end approaching, he had hollowed a shallow trench in the loose earth for his own resting place, and, lying in it, had drawn a few green boughs over himself. On his breast, beneath his crossed hands, lay a broad strip of birch bark. On this he had laboriously carved, in verse, the pitiful story of his last deeds and thoughts. This Death Song has become famous as the " Lament of Cadieux," and is still sung by the Canadian *voyageurs* to a melancholy air which they themselves have adapted to it. The " Lament," in spite of metrical imperfections, is sufficiently touching, and is given below on account of the strikingly tragic circumstances under which it was composed.

    LA COMPLAINTE DE CADIEUX.

Petit rocher de la haute montagne,
Je viens finir ici cette campagne !
Ah ! doux échos, entendez mes soupirs ;
En languissant je vais bientot mourir !

Petits oiseaux, vos douces harmonies,
Quand vous chantez, me rattach' à la vie :
Ah ! si j' avais des ailes comme vous,
Je s'rais heureux avant qu'il fut deux jours !

Seul en ces bois, que j'ai eu de soucis !
Pensant toujours à mes si chers amis,
Je demandais : Hélas ! sont-ils noyés ?
Les Iroquois les auraient-ils tués ?

Un des ces jours que, m'étant éloigné,
En revenant je vis une fumée ;
Je me suis dit : Ah ! grand Dieu, qu'est ceci ?
Les Iroquois m'ont-ils pris mon logis ?

Je me suis mis un peu à l'ambassade,
Afin de voir si c'était embuscade ;
Alors je vis trois visages Français !—
M'ont mis le coeur, d'une trop grande joie !

Mes genoux plient, ma faible voix s'arrête,
Je tombe—Hélas ! à partir ils s'apprêtent :
Je reste seul—Pas un qui me console,
Quand la mort vient par un si grand désole !

Un loup hurlant vint près de ma cabane
Voir si mon feu n'avait plus de boucane ;
Je lui ai dit : Retire-toi d'ici ;
Car, par ma foi, je perc'rai ton habit !

Un noir corbeau, volant à l'aventure,
Vient se percher tout près de ma toiture :
Je lui ai dit : Mangeur de chair humaine,
Va-t'en chercher autre viande que mienne.

Va-t'en là-bas, dans ces bois et marais,
Tu trouveras plusieurs corps iroquois :
Tu trouveras des chairs, aussi des os ;
Va-t'en plus loin, laisse-moi en repos !

Rossignolet va dire à ma maitresse,
A mes enfants, qu'un adieu je leur laisse ;
Que j'ai gardé mon amour et ma foi,
Et désormais faut renoncer à moi !

C'est donc ici que le mond' m'abandonne !—
Mais j'ai secours en vous Sauveur des hommes !
Très-Sainte Vierge, ah ! m'abandonnez pas,
Permettez-mois d' mourir entre vos bras !

CHAPTER IV.

THE STORY OF PHILEMON WRIGHT.

Philemon Wright——The Father of the Ottawa——A Native of Woburn, Mass.——His Four Visits to Canada——Fixes on the Chaudière for Settlement——Organizes His Colony at Woburn——Their Winter Journey——Hardships and Adventures——In the Woods——On the Ice——A Good Indian——The Chaudière reached, 7th March, 1800——First Experiences——More Indians——Not so Good——Peace prevails——An Early Spring——Bountiful Crops——Square Timber for Quebec——Glimpses at Settlement in 1824——Philemon's Death in 1839——Anecdote of Lord Aylmer——The Fortune of Nicholas Sparks ——Alonzo Wright, M.P., the "King of the Gatineau."

From 1763 until 1796, no important travellers visited the Chaudière. In the latter year, Philemon Wright, an enterprising resident of Woburn, near Boston, Massachusetts, made his first exploration of the River Ottawa, with the deliberate plan of laying the foundations of a new settlement, some day to be a town. The city of Hull is for all practical purposes as much a part of the

Canadian capital now, as Southwark was a part of London for a long time before the County Council brought them together. It was on the site of Hull that our pioneer, four years later, planted his hearth, and became in deed and name, "the Father of the Ottawa." His story is a remarkable one, and was related by himself in 1820, before a committee of the House of Assembly of Lower Canada. It is a striking picture of indomitable courage and perseverance crowned with brilliant success. In this instance, the dream of the pioneer has been realized, and in Canada to-day there are countless opportunities for the repetition of his enterprise, and the achievement of a like success. For that reason, as well as for the intrinsic interest of the narrative, the reader will be asked to follow the main incidents of Philemon Wright's career after he came to Canada.

At the time of his first visit, above referred to, he was thirty-six years of age, and married, with a large family of children for

CHOOSING A SITE.

whom he wished to provide on a larger scale than the prospects of a Massachusetts farmer could promise. In 1797, he again visited Canada, and examined the country from Quebec to Montreal, on both sides of the St. Lawrence, and then up the Ottawa, or Grand River, as far as the Chaudière Falls. He studied both the navigation of the latter river, and its fitness for settlement. He found that the total distance from the junction of the Ottawa with the St. Lawrence at Montreal, to the Chaudière, was 120 miles. Some sparse settlement existed for the first forty-five miles, up to the Long Sault Rapids. Beyond that, the seventy-five or eighty miles was a complete wilderness. At the upper end of the rapids there was a stretch of sixty-four miles of still water, extending to the Chaudière, sufficiently deep, as he said, "to float a sloop of war." He found that this part of the country was entirely unknown to the inhabitants of Montreal, though its immense resources in fine timber "were sufficient to furnish supplies for any foreign market, even to load a thousand vessels." Many thousand vessels have since been loaded with Ottawa timber. Again, in 1798, this persevering but cautious man paid his third visit to his future home, and returned to Massachusetts, with a full determination to commence the settlement. He failed, however, to inspire his neighbours with his own confidence in the scheme, and he therefore selected two respectable men from among them, and hired them to go with him the next summer, to examine and report upon what they saw. They reached the Chaudière on the 1st of October, 1799, and spent twenty days exploring the lands on the north side of the river. They do not seem to have paid the slightest attention to the wild cliffs and forbidding precipices on the opposite shore. They climbed to the tops of more than one hundred trees to view the situation of the country and the character of the timber, from which they were able also to judge of the nature of the soil.

The report made upon their return, by these explorers, was so satisfactory to the people of Woburn that Mr. Wright was able to hire as many men as he wished for his new settlement.

It was a far cry from Boston to Hull in the winter of 1799-1800, but the nineteenth century was only a month old when the little colony braved the journey. Their leader, determined to assume all the risks himself, had hired about twenty-five men and purchased mill-irons, axes, scythes, hoes, and all other necessary tools. He tells us that he also "brought fourteen horses and eight oxen, seven sleighs, and five families, together with a number of barrels of clear pork, destitute of bone, of my own raising." The party arrived in Montreal in eight days, without mishap. They soon started from there, and while they were among the settlements they found beaten roads for the first forty miles up the Ottawa, and they made about fifteen miles each day.

After this there were no roads, and the snow was nearly two feet deep in the bush. A party of axemen had to cut out a road before the sleighs, and it took three or four days to do the sixteen miles to pass the Long Sault Rapids. The description of their night encampments is worth giving in Wright's own language: "We fixed upon some spot near water to encamp for the night, particularly observing that there were no big trees to fall upon us, or our cattle, and if there were, to cut them down. Then we cleared away the snow and cut down trees for fire for the whole night, the women and children sleeping in covered sleighs, and the men with blankets, around the fire, and the cattle made fast to the standing trees. In this situation, about thirty of us spent the night; and I must say that I never saw men more cheerful and happy, in my life, than they seemed to be—having no landlord to call upon us for our expenses, nor to complain of our extravagances, nor no dirty floor to sleep upon, but the sweet ground which belonged to our ancient sovereign."

It is to be remembered that this was a party of Americans who had recently severed all connection with their "ancient sovereign," to whose paternal protection they were now returning. Philemon Wright did not come to Canada on any sentimental grounds, as did so many United Empire Loyalists, who would not live under the Republic. Indeed, although at the time but a lad of sixteen, he had fought against his "ancient sovereign," at Bunker Hill.

When the party arrived at the stretches of the river above the rapids, they travelled upon the ice, but progress was slow, as, even there, the snow lay over a foot deep. Each night they camped upon the shore, before a blazing fire, and before daylight they cooked their breakfast and the provisions for the day, and so made an early start. During their first day upon the ice, they met an Indian and his wife, drawing a child upon a little bark sleigh (toboggan). The savages were lost in admiration at the oxen and horses, and the outfit generally, but not one word could either party understand from the other. At length, of his own accord, the Indian seemed to take pity upon the helplessness of the cattle, and, sending his wife off to the woods, placed himself in front of the sleighs, led the way, and tried the ice with his hatchet every few feet. This he continued to do every day until the Chaudière was reached, on the 7th of March, and after receiving a few presents, he started down the river alone to find his wife and child somewhere in the woods, sixty miles away.

The busy axes of the pioneers soon hewed enough logs, and comfortable houses for all were built. While thus engaged, an incident occurred which made it necessary for Wright to invoke the name of his "ancient sovereign," King George, to some purpose. The chiefs of a neighbouring tribe had been for some days inspecting all that was done, with a deep and friendly interest, and cheerfully shared the cup of convivial rum. They also did a little trading with their maple-sugar and venison. In about ten days time, however, they made a stern demand through an interpreter, to know what authority the settlers had for cutting down their wood and taking their land. They feared the destruction of the forests and game, of sugaries and beaver huts and all their means of subsistence. Wright assured them that he had the fullest authority from their Great Father, who lived on the other side of the water, to take these lands, and that it was in order also, to help the Indians to get goods and trade without going to Montreal. Still unsatisfied, they had to be paid a small sum to buy out their sugar-kettles, etc., but when they also received a message from the Indian department that the settlement was duly authorized, they became so friendly as to create Wright a brother chief. They crowned him, kissed him, dined him, buried the hatchet, and they all lived happily ever after.

To the surprise of all, spring opened much earlier than they had ever known it in Massachusetts, and they cleared enough land the first season to raise plenty of vegetables—as much as 1,000 bushels of potatoes. The cattle thrived by browsing on the buds of trees, and the richness of the soil was extraordinary. In the second year, 3,000 bushels of fine wheat were raised, forty bushels growing to the acre. Every year more land was cleared, more barns and mills were built. By 1804, a smithy, shoemaker's shop, tailor's shop, bake-house, and tannery were in operation. The greatest achievement of Mr. Wright, however, was when, in 1807, he took the first raft of square timber from Hull to Quebec. He was 35 days in getting the raft down the Long Sault Rapids, which can often be run by a raft now in twenty-four hours. He took it by the new channel, north of the

Island of Montreal, and thus brought it more cheaply to Quebec than he could have taken it to Montreal. After this he derived a large and an unfailing income from his rafts of square timber.

We will look in again upon this settlement, in 1824, and see how our friend, Philemon Wright, has fared. He tells us that more than once he was burned out without insurance, and often had lost nearly all his property except his land and the conserved energy of his ever-flowing waterpower. Yet, in this year, we find him the owner of four large farms with 3,000 acres cleared. He is making annually 1,100 tons of hay, and has 756 acres in grain and roots, with stock and pasturage in proportion. His buildings alone are valued at $75,000; and his farm, stock, and buildings at a quarter of a million. It is not necessary to pursue the story of increased and uninterrupted prosperity, which followed this brave and worthy man until the day of his death, in 1839.

A good story is told of him while he was at Quebec, as a member of the lower Canada Legislature, in 1833. The Governor, Lord Aylmer, invited Mr. Wright and a number of his colleagues to a dinner. He promptly arrived at the Chateau at noon—his usual hour for dinner. His Excellency received him with the greatest politeness, and they sat down to breakfast together. On saying goodbye, the Governor said, "You're coming to dinner, are you not Mr. Wright?" Observing that his blunder had dawned on Wright for the first time, His Excellency relieved his embarrassment by saying: "You know, Mr. Wright, I shall consider myself fortunate to meet so interesting a man as yourself, twice in one day."

While the element of chance did not form a basis for Philemon Wright's prosperity, the early settlement of Ottawa furnished a remarkable instance of a large fortune made by sheer good luck. One of Wright's employees, Nicholas Sparks, had an opportunity to buy, at a bargain, a large tract of land among the rocks and gullies and cliffs of the wild land opposite Hull. He drew all his wages and, by borrowing a little more from his employer, was able to secure this propperty. Soon afterwards, the Royal Engineers laid out the large works of the Rideau Canal in the midst of his land, and purchased from him, at a good price, what they required for the canal, and also a quantity of other land. Sparks at once turned the rest of his farm into a town plot, and was able to sell it at his own prices, because he controlled the situation. The " Regent Street " of the Canadian capital now bears his name, and he, in many ways, promoted the town's prosperity, and left a handsome heritage to his children.

A grandson of Philemon Wright—Alonzo—for many years represented, in the Canadian Parliament, the large constituency in the province of Quebec, which included the city of Hull. He was a notable figure in the

House. His culture and wit were only equalled by the princely hospitality which he extended to his fellow members at his country residence, on the banks of the Gatineau river, some five miles out of town. He was known far and wide as the "King of the Gatineau." He did not live long after his retirement from public life in 1891, and the name of "Wright" has been given to a new constituency to commemorate the worthy family—the pioneers of that district.

CHAPTER V.

HOW OTTAWA BECAME THE CAPITAL OF CANADA.

Quebec Capital until 1791——Colony divided——Toronto Capital of Upper Canada——Kingston First Choice, 1841——Dickens describes the Place——Montreal selected in 1843——Mob burn Parliament Buildings——Alternate Sittings at Toronto and Quebec——The Queen asked to select Permanent Site——Ottawa chosen——Voted against by Legislature in 1858——Favoured in 1859——Prince of Wales lays Foundation Stone——First Session held there in 1866——Became Federal Capital of the Confederation.

Quebec had been the capital of the old Province of Canada from before the days of the conquest until the "Constitutional Act" was passed in England, in 1791. This legislation divided the old colony into the two Provinces of Upper and Lower Canada; the capital of the latter remained at Quebec, and Toronto became the capital of the former. When the Imperial Act, of 1840, reunited the two Provinces, it was left to the Governor-

General to select the new capital of United Canada. In accordance with this provision the seat of Government was fixed by Lord Sydenham at Kingston. In the second session the members of the Legislative Assembly, by a vote of two to one, decided that it was not a desirable place for the capital. In that year Charles Dickens paid the place a visit, and gave a dismal picture of it. " Indeed," said he, " it may be said of Kingston that one-half of it appears to be burnt down, and the other half not built up." Little did he foresee the handsome and populous city of fifty years later. However, the hostility of members continued, and on the 3rd of November, 1843, Montreal was chosen as the seat of government by a vote of 51 to 27.

The honour of being the capital did not restrain Montreal from sadly misbehaving itself in 1849. Differing in a marked manner from the views of the majority of the Legislature upon an important Bill before that body, an excited mob sacked and burnt down the

Parliament House, and insulted and attacked the Governor-General, Lord Elgin. The Assembly promptly passed an address praying His Excellency to call Parliament alternately at Toronto and Quebec, every four years.

The perambulating system failed to satisfy any one, and after much squabbling a resolution was finally carried on the 24th March, 1857, in favour of an address to Her Majesty praying her to select the seat of government. This Her Majesty did, and fixed upon Ottawa. In making the choice, the Queen was guided by the advice of the Governor-General, Sir Edmund Head, whose judgment was influenced by the idea that this was the safest settlement of a dangerous question. Apart from the political advantages of the location, the magnificence of the site for a capital is said to have impressed Sir Edmund very favourably.

The Queen's decision became known early in 1858, and created intense local hostility in the other sections of the Province. The Assembly again increased the difficulty by passing a resolution on the 28th of July, 1858: " That it is the opinion of this House that the City of Ottawa ought not to be the permanent seat of Government for the Province." However, the same Assembly, in February, 1859, after an excited discussion, and by a small, but sufficient majority, affirmed Her Majesty's decision, and Ottawa at last became the Canadian capital.

Before the close of the year the work of construction was begun upon the Parliament Buildings, and the ceremony of laying the corner stone was conducted with great solemnity by the Prince of Wales, on the 1st of September, 1860. During the Autumn of the year 1865, the public departments were removed from Quebec to Ottawa, and the buildings were ready for the meeting of the last session of the Provincial Parliament on the 8th June, 1866. When Confederation became an accomplished fact in 1867, the buildings were taken over as the Federal Capital of the Dominion.

CHAPTER VI.

THE NATIONAL BUILDINGS.

Imposing Appearance—Anthony Trollope's Praise of Them—Charles Dudley Warner's Opinion of Them—Form a Large Quadrangle—The Lovers' Walk—The Terrace—Electric Light in Tower while House in Session—Pure Gothic of Older Buildings—Beautiful Colour of Stone—Italian Renaissance in newest Building—The Library—External Grace and Interior Beauty—Senate and Commons Chambers—Speaker's Apartments—Galleries—Pages—Story of an Applicant—Offices of Governor-General and Different Ministers—Experimental Farm—Supreme and Exchequer Courts.

Approaching the Capital from any point, the National Buildings are seen towering above the roofs and steeples of the town. When they were far from possessing the imposing beauty of to-day, an English traveller gave them his unstinted praise. Anthony Trollope wrote of the Parliament Buildings as he saw them, in 1861, in this fashion:

"It stands nobly on a magnificent river, with high, overhanging rock, and a natural grandeur of position which has perhaps gone far in recommending it to those whose voice in the matter has been potential. Having the world of Canada from whence to chose the site of a new town, the choosers have certainly chosen well. . . . . The glory of Ottawa will be—and, indeed, already is—the set of public buildings which is now being erected on the rock which guards, as it were, the town from the river. I take it upon myself to say that as regards purity of art and manliness of conception the work is entitled to the very highest praise. . . . . I have no hesitation in risking my reputation for judgment in giving my warmest commendation to them as regards beauty of outline and truthful nobility of detail. . . . . I know no modern Gothic purer of its kind, or less sullied with fictitious ornamentation, and I know no site for such a set of buildings so happy as regards both beauty and grandeur."

Another visitor told us what he thought

Parliament and Library Buildings—From the West.

of the place in 1889. Any words of commendation from Charles Dudley Warner will be accepted as representing the judgment of one of the unquestioned leaders of American thought and taste. He writes : " The beauty and attraction of the city are due to the concentration here of political interest. The situation on the bluffs of the Ottawa River is commanding, and gives fine opportunity for architectural display. The group of Government Buildings is surpassingly fine. The Parliament House and the Department Buildings, on three sides of a square, are exceedingly effective in color, and the perfection of Gothic details, especially in the noble towers. There are few groups of buildings anywhere so pleasing to the eye, or that appeal more strongly to one's sense of dignity and beauty."

The Parliament Buildings proper provide accommodation for the Senate and the House of Commons, and the Library is so near as to form a portion of them. The Eastern, Western and Southern blocks are Departmental

Buildings, and enclose a vast quadrangle, which is laid out in walks and drives and spacious lawns. Drives and walks also encircle the buildings, and one of the latter is the famous Lovers' Walk, which is carried along among the rocks and trees upon the side of the high cliff overlooking the river, and affords a lovely promenade nearly half a mile in length. The grounds occupied by the National Buildings are some thirty acres in extent, and on three sides command views up and down the river, with the wooded Laurentian Hills in the distance. The Terrace, which sweeps round the north side of the Parliament Buildings and Library, goes to the very edge of the cliff, and affords a prospect of unrivalled beauty.

From the top of the tower of the main building there flashes at night, while the House is in session, a powerful electric light. Over the town and over the great basin of the Ottawa Valley this beacon flames out the signal to farm and hamlet, for twenty miles around, that the representatives of the people are

WESTERN DEPARTMENTAL BLOCK, AND MACKENZIE TOWER.

keeping their weary vigils. It may be that it brings to the mind of many a citizen the thought that, after all, the life of an M.P. is not a happy one, and that the honours are dearly bought at the price of absence from home, and of many sleepless nights.

The original structures consisted of the Parliamentary and Library buildings, and the Eastern block as they now exist, and part of the Western block. These are a pure Gothic of no particular period, but the noble civic buildings of the Low Countries and Italy are understood to have afforded suggestions to the architects. At a later date the Western Departmental block was much enlarged, and the magnificent Mackenzie tower was added to it. This rises to a height of 272 feet, and eclipses the tower in the main building, which is 255 feet high. The style of these additions is Gothic of a similar character but of a later date. The effective rock-faced work of the walls is generally of sandstone from the Nepean quarries close to Ottawa. Its colouring is varied and beautiful, and grows in richness under the hand of time. The dressings are of Ohio sandstone brought from that State, and the red arches are of Potsdam sandstone obtained from St. Lawrence County, in New York State.

It has been an old and pleasant fancy to trace the origin of the pointed Gothic arch back to a reverent imitation of the graceful branches of the elm, bowing together in the shadowy glades of the European forests. It was there that the supposed barbarian inventors of this architecture had found their shrines, before raising Christian temples in long-enduring stone. A keen observer of Art and Nature has drawn the writer's attention to the striking resemblance which this group of Ottawa buildings presents, when viewed from a distance, to a forest of giant pine trees. To illustrate his point, he has instanced the fact that there is a grove of large pines a few miles down the river, which stand out against the sky, and might easily be mistaken, in twilight or in mist, for the Parliament Buildings. No wonder that the alert mind of this artistic friend (Sir William Van Horne) propounded the theory, that if Gothic interiors and arches owe so much to the elm, the glorious irregularities of Gothic tower and spire and pinnacle reflect an inspiration received from the grandeur and majesty of the pine.

The Southern Departmental block is separated from the other buildings by Wellington Street, and is built in an entirely different style, being a modification of Italian Renaissance, and its material is sandstone from Newcastle, New Brunswick. The change from the Gothic was made in order to gain more space and light in the offices.

The Library building is a rotunda in form, but possesses a marvellous combination of strength and grace. The great height of the dome is supported by massive buttresses, and by flying buttresses, which are lightened by graceful pinnacles. The interior is equally imposing. From the floor to the centre of the dome is 140 feet, while the height of Westminster Hall is only 90 feet. The floor is inlaid with Canadian woods, and the bookshelves are richly carved in Canadian white pine, rising to three stories, with galleries for access to the books. The library contains 180,000 volumes, and is supported by a Parliamentary grant.

The Chambers for the Senate and for the House of Commons are identical in size, shape and design, both having a length of 88 feet and a width of 47 feet. Their general appearance is very different. The carpets and upholstering in the Senate are red, while the treatment in the Commons is green. In the Commons the Speaker's chair is at one side of the Chamber, while in the Senate the Throne and Speaker's chair are at the north end. The floor space in the popular House is rather crowded by the chairs and desks of 213 members, while the Upper House gives larger space and more roomy desks to its 81 members. While the supplying of desks and writing materials to members in their separate seats is calculated to secure a fuller attendance than in the English Houses, it has a distinct tendency to encourage the writing out and the use of long notes, and the consequent length and tediousness of speeches. It is almost fatal to "debate" of the best parliamentary order. As necessary adjuncts to both Chambers there are a number of committee rooms and offices for the officials and for large staffs of clerks. The Press is provided with good rooms and their own gallery, while the postoffice, the Clerk of the Crown in Chancery, the law clerks, the French translators, the Hansard men and telegraph operators, all have their separate quarters. There are reading rooms, smoking rooms, restaurants and private dining rooms for each House, and some dozen rooms are assigned to ministers and leading members for use during the session. The Speakers of both Houses have handsome suites of apartments, adjoining the Chambers, and these are more or less the scenes of hospitable gatherings. Residential apartments are also furnished in the building to Black Rod in the Senate and the Sergeant-at-Arms in the Commons, In the popular House there is always a large attendance in the galleries, which extend all round the Chamber, when any question of interest is to be discussed, or any good speaker is expected to take the floor. The Canadian woman is not caged in behind bars after the cruel example of her Westminster prototype, but she has equal rights in all places where men may go. Under careful regulations different galleries may be used. There are the Speaker's Gallery for the wives and families of a select few, the Senators' Gallery for the exclusive use of the Canadian peers and those whom they desire to honour, the Visitors' Gallery and the Ladies' Gallery, for which tickets are given out daily by the Sergeant-at-Arms, the Deputy Minister's Gallery, and the Public Galleries. On some occasions as many as a thousand visitors to the gallery honour the legislators with their presence. It has been insinuated that there are parliamentary performers who can always " play " better to a good house than to empty galleries.

If a member in his place wishes to mail a letter, get a book from the Library, a glass of water or a new pen, he snaps his fingers and a little page, neatly clad in Eton jacket and dark clothes, flies to do his bidding. There are some twenty of these little chaps, and half of them are in attendance in the Chamber night and day. When there is a late sitting the poor little fellows become very tired, and often fall asleep on the steps to the Speaker's chair. The choice of these pages is made by the Speaker, assisted by the Sergeant-at-Arms, and they are nearly always the sons of widows to whom their pay is an object. It is not fine, big boys that are required, but smart little boys. As several of the best pages outgrow their usefulness every year, vacancies are continually occurring, and it is sometimes too amusing to hear the mothers' assurances that their sons are nice and small for their age. An anxious parent has been discovered placing her offspring behind a chair, and directing him to bend his legs "with intent to deceive" the keen eye of the Sergeant-at-Arms as to his height.

In the Eastern Departmental block are the offices of the Governor-General and his staff, and the Privy Council Chamber where Cabinet councils are held. The ministers, whose departments are in the Eastern block, are: The President of the Queen's Privy Council (the Premier now holding that office), the Minister of Justice, the Minister of Finance, the Secretary of State and the Solicitor-General.

In the Western block the following ministers have their departments: the Minister of Marine and Fisheries, the Minister of Railways and Canals, the Minister of Public Works, the Minister of Trade and Commerce, the Minister of Militia and Defence, the Minister of Customs and the Minister of Inland Revenue.

In the Southern block are the offices of the Postmaster-General, the Minister of Agriculture, the Minister of the Interior and the Superintendent-General of Indian Affairs.

The Patent Office is attached to the Department of Agriculture, and is in the Southern block. The offices of the Mounted Police and of the Archives are in the Western block, and the Auditor-General exercises his independent sway in the Eastern block. The Geological and Natural History Survey is attached to the Department of the Interior, but has its offices and its splendid museum about a quarter of a mile from the Southern block in the old barracks in Sussex Street.

Under the Department of Agriculture there are five Experimental Farms in various parts of Canada. The first was established by the purchase of five hundred acres of land in the immediate neighborhood of the Capital, which is known as the "Central Farm," and is in complete working order. Besides the Director, there are a number of highly-educated resident officials who conduct operations in the most scientific manner for the purpose of experiments as to soils, fertilizers, seeds, cattle, horses, sheep, swine, poultry, fruit trees, vegetables and dairying. Not only is the information of results spread among the farmers of the country, but samples of all seeds deemed worthy of introduction are sent out. Among the officials are an agriculturist, a dairy commissioner, an entomologist, a botanist, a chemist, a horticulturist and a poultry manager. The buildings and appliances are most complete, and are the delight of all visitors who take an interest in any sort of work that can be done on a farm, from wheat-raising to bee-keeping.

Under a bank which slopes down from the western front of the Western block is an unpretentious building of Nepean sandstone which shelters the Supreme Court of the Dominion and the Exchequer Court. The Supreme Court is the highest Canadian Court and has appellate criminal and civil jurisdiction throughout the Dominion. It consists of a Chief Justice and five Puisne Judges, who reside at Ottawa.

The Exchequer Court is presided over by a single judge, and has original exclusive jurisdiction in all actions against the Crown.

These are federal courts, but in each province there is a complete judicial system. From all Canadian Courts an appeal can be taken before that great Imperial tribunal, the Judicial Committee of the Privy Council.

CHAPTER VII.

THE CANADIAN SYSTEM OF GOVERNMENT.

The Charter in British North America Act, 1867—Similar in Principle to that of the United Kingdom—Prepared by Canadians—Conceded by England, wisely—First American Convention of 1774 differently treated—Canadian Rights of Taxation yielded by England—Senate and House of Commons of Canada—Constitution and Popular Representation—Provincial Legislatures—Most Second Provincial Chambers abolished—Lieutenant Governors of Provinces—Their Loyalty to British System, though Hostile Cabinets forced upon Them—Division of Legislative Powers between the Dominion and Provinces—Difficulties as to Educational matters—Framers of Canadian Constitution alarmed at American Civil War and Extreme Doctrine of State Sovereignty—Residuary Legislative Powers left in Dominion, not Provinces—American Constitution separates Executive from Legislative Powers—Canada follows Modern English Doctrine—House of Commons Controls Executive—President's Message compared with Governor General's Speech—Political Leadership of Speaker of House of Representatives justified by Miss Follett—Her Views of Defects of American System—English System First grafted on Federal Governments in Case of Canada—Canadian Constitution, in 1867, granted to a larger Population than the American Constitution in 1787—On Full Consideration Canada chose the English Model.

The Charter and Constitution of the Dominion is the Imperial British North America Act of 1867. To create the machinery for a Federal and a number of Provincial Governments required many clauses, but the real charter of Canadian liberty is to be found in the first sentence of the Act, which recites that the Dominion shall have "a constitution similar in principle to that of the United Kingdom."

This Act was prepared by Canadian statesmen, approved by the Colonial Legislatures, and, at their request, passed into law by the paramount Parliament of the Empire. Not a line of it was forced upon an unwilling legislature by the British Parliament. A complete system of self-government was claimed and frankly yielded. It was a bold but a far-seeing policy for England to trust her greatest Colonies "all in all."

The mind reverts to other days when other Colonies sent delegates to Philadelphia, in 1774, instructed "to procure the return of that harmony and union so beneficial to the whole Empire and so ardently desired by all British America." It was, however, too early for

British statesmen of the calibre of Grenville and Townshend and North to advise an unwilling king to yield to the Colonies the right to place all taxes on themselves.

In 1867, British statesmen and parliament conceded, without hesitation, to Canada the rights, not only to tax herself, but to levy taxes as heavy as she chose upon the imports from the Motherland. Of this permission she has most freely availed herself.

In the Federal Parliament at Ottawa there are two Chambers, the Senate and the House of Commons. All measures to become law must be passed by both Houses, and, as in England, must receive the assent of the Crown, which is signified by Her Majesty's representative, the Governor-General. The Senators are practically life Peers, appointed as new Peers are in England, by the government of the day, and therefore they do not possess the strength or influence that attaches to the House of Commons, which is elected by the Canadian people for a term of five years, subject to

Hon. C. A. P. Pelletier, C.M.G., P.C.
The Speaker, Senate of Canada.

BASIS OF REPRESENTATION.

dissolution at any time by the Crown on advice of responsible ministers. The representation in the House of Commons is based strictly on population as shown by each decennial census, while in the Senate the membership is not changed by the shifting of population, but has been arranged to give a fixed representation to Provinces. There are 81 Senators, and 213 members of the Commons. Bills for appropriating any part of the public revenue, or for imposing any tax or impost, must originate in the House of Commons. The property qualification for members of the House of Commons has been abolished, and the franchise of those who elect them has been gradually extended until it has almost reached the point of manhood suffrage.

After a decennial census the number of members to be returned to the Commons from different Provinces is liable to change, except in the case of Quebec where the representation is fixed at 65. Each of the other Provinces is entitled to such a number of members as will bear the same proportion to the number of its population as the number 65 bears to the number of the population of Quebec.

As a result of the census of 1891, the House of Commons now stands:—

From	Ontario	92	members.
"	Quebec	65	"
"	Nova Scotia	20	"
"	New Brunswick..	14	"
"	Manitoba	7	"
"	British Columbia..	6	"
"	Prince Edward I...	5	"
"	North-west Ter...	4	"

Total number of M.P.'s 213

Among the Quebec members there are 49 French, and from the other Provinces but 4 are French.

There are Provincial Legislatures in each of the Provinces, but second chambers do not exist among them elsewhere than in Quebec and Nova Scotia. They were either left out by the Canadian framers of the British North

America Act, or the Provinces have themselves felt that they were expensive luxuries and have abolished them. All legislation of the Provinces must receive the assent of the Crown, which is represented there, for all Provincial purposes, by the Lieutenant-Governors. These high officers are appointed for a term of five years by the Dominion ministry, and, like the Governor-General in the Federal sphere, they are to administer affairs through constitutional advisers who possess the confidence of their popular chambers. Curious results follow. There are to-day in several Provinces Lieutenant-Governors who were active politicians when appointed, and who have ever since been acting loyally in all respects under the advice of their ministers, although these are politicians of an opposite and hostile party. Public opinion would not tolerate anything else, for we are proud of and determined to maintain in spirit and in letter, in theory and in practice, a "constitution similar in principle to that of the United Kingdom."

When the Provincial delegates met in conference at Quebec to frame a Federal constitution perhaps their greatest difficulty was to arrive at a division of legislative powers between the National and the Provincial legislative bodies.

By sections 91 and 92 of the B.N.A. Act a careful division of legislative powers has been made. In a general sense exclusive authority has been given to the Federal body over Trade and Commerce, Navigation and Shipping, the Tariff, the Militia, Indian affairs, Interest, Marriage and Divorce, and the Criminal Law. On the other hand each Province has exclusive legislative jurisdiction over Property and Civil Rights, Administration of Justice, and Constitution of Courts within the Province, Local Works and Municipal Institutions. In regard to Education, the Provincial powers are restricted somewhat by a right of appeal to the Dominion, which has been given to religious minorities, who may be dissatisfied with local legislation by which they are affected. This

Southern Departmental Block, Ottawa.

mixed jurisdiction is a menace to the peace of Confederation, as it has already given an opening for dangerous agitations in the case of New Brunswick and Manitoba School Laws.

The Quebec Conference met to consider a plan of Federal Union just at the close of the Civil War in the United States, and were impressed by the danger to a Federal Government if its constitution could be interpreted in favour of State sovereignty and implied rights of secession. The clause of the American Constitution which creates the reserved sovereignties of the States is in these words: "The powers not delegated to the United States by the Constitution, nor prohibited by it to the States, are reserved to the States respectively or to the people." The framers of the Canadian Constitution reversed the American plan of distribution of the residuary legislative powers by providing that the Dominion Parliament "may make laws for the peace, order and good government of Canada in relation to all matters not coming within the classes of subjects by this Act assigned exclusively to the legislatures of the Provinces."

It may not be unreasonable to hope that the Canadian plan adds a strength and dignity to the central authority, which in times of trial shall bind together the elements of her nationality.

There is another feature of the Canadian Constitution which differs *toto cœlo* from that of the United States. We have followed in strictness the English system (as it is found to-day) of Parliamentary Government. That system needs no defence since it has been followed as closely as possible by almost every European country which has adopted representative institutions. When the American Constitution was framed, in 1787, the English institutions were not developed, and could not have been followed. The great authorities in those days upon the British Constitution were Blackstone, De Lolme and Montesquieu. These writers had failed to perceive the steady downfall of the royal power that was in progress, and their theories were based upon the old practices of government under the Stuarts. They laid it down as the theory of the English system that there should be a complete separation between the Executive, Legislative and Judicial functions. They did not appreciate that there had been already going on a gradual displacement of the executive power from the sovereign to the responsible Ministers, who have now simply become a committee of the House of Commons. Canadians have recognized and adopted these changed conditions. Every executive act is subject to be criticized and, it may be, condemned by the House of Commons. All important legislation of Parliament is initiated or controlled by the Executive, who must be represented there by leading ministers. The Sovereign must dismiss any administration censured by the House of Commons, and must find advisers who are acceptable to that paramount body. Thus have the executive and the legislative functions become inextricably blended. The executive is kept in harmony with the popular body, and the laws passed by the popular body must be in harmony with the policy of the executive for the time being. The fathers of the American Constitution followed the theories of the text-books, and provided for a rigid separation between the executive and the legislative powers. The President with advisers, or secretaries, is the Executive, and he has no power of initiating or controlling the legislation of Congress, as the latter has no effective power of censuring his executive acts. A President's message may be of interest as giving the personal views of a prominent statesman upon public affairs, but even when his party happens to control both the Senate and the House of Representatives there is no guarantee that his advice as to legislation will be adopted. If either House is in the hands of an opposite party his message cannot be said to influence legislation more than the considered utterances of any other public man. The speech from the Throne, placed in the hands of the Governor-General in Canada by his Ministers, contains an outline of policy and legislation which cannot be ignored by the House of Commons. The existence of the administration is staked upon the approval and adoption of that address by the representatives of the people.

The President's independence of Congress is approved of by many American writers, but the want of responsible political leaders in the House of Representatives is deplored by other thoughtful students of the Constitution. Curious devices have been gradually adopted to get over this latter difficulty. The Speakership of the House of Representatives has fast become changed (shall we say " degraded " ?) into a political leadership. Not only is this the case but it is boldly justified as being urgently required. In Miss Follett's recent and very able book she states the case clearly and well. She says : " The House of Commons does its business under the direction of the Ministry, and some way must be found of concentrating both power and responsibility in the House of

Representatives." And again: "Next to the lack of harmony in legislation the greatest evil of our Government, and one almost universally recognized, is the difficulty of knowing whom to hold accountable." One more extract will suffice. Miss Follet says: "There is, however, need of far greater unity in legislative initiative. The two great and acknowledged defects of our present political system are: first, lack of legislative leadership; and, secondly, the lack of connection between executive and legislature."

While the whole world acknowledges the many admirable features of the American Constitution, it may be pardonable in a Canadian to be proud to find it thus pointed out that, in some respects at least, our own Constitution is admittedly the better of the two.

It was a new experiment when the Canadian statesmen ventured to engraft upon their proposed Federal Government, and all its separate Provincial autonomies, the English system that belonged to a single monarchical state; a system, too, which had been of recent growth in England, where freedom had broadened " slowly down from precedent to precedent." Only thirty years have tested the strength of our system, yet it has so far been equal to the requirements of government. It was a landmark in history when the fathers of the American Constitution, in 1787, framed a plan for a federal union of separate States of great area, and with a population of 3,639,000 souls. Was it not an event of some importance when the fathers of the Canadian Constitution, in 1864-67, framed their plan for a federal union of separate Provinces of still greater area, and with a population of 3,686,000 souls?

The two systems of free government are, for weal or for woe, side by side on this continent. The Canadian plan was adopted after eighty years of the American Union had shown it to be equal to fearful strains. Yet we thought many lessons were to be learned from those eighty years. We saw that, after the peaceful revolution worked by the Reform Bill of 1832, England had placed herself well in the front of the democracies of the world, and we therefore chose, as our Charter says, "a Constitution similar in principle to that of the United Kingdom."

Commons of Canada Interior.

CHAPTER VIII.

THE HOUSE OF COMMONS.

The House of Commons controls Executive——Its Influence in Legislation——Foreign Relations often Involved——French Treaty——Copyright——Relations with the United States——Examples——American Alien Labor Law——Danger of Retaliation——Mr. W. T. Stead's Views of Canada's Position——Her Power and Responsibility——Colonial Jingoism——Questions of Great Diversity dealt with——Vast Distances in Canada——Compared with Distances from London——And in the United States——Confidence in Our Future——Leadership of the House——When Premier is in the Senate——Recent Instances——Leader of the Opposition——Important Functions of Leaders——Their Great Power——Conduct of Business in the House——English Precedents followed——Reasons for Closure in England, but not in Canada——Long Sittings in England——Longer in Canada——Continuous Sitting for a Week In 1896——Forms and Ceremonies——Black Rod——Sergeant-at-Arms and the Mace.

The House of Commons is the centre of political power, as it can make or unmake Ministries by its vote. Its authority over the Executive is thus absolute, and by reason of its control over money bills, and its directly representative character, it is altogether more powerful than the Senate as a legislative body. The interests involved in its debates sometimes extend to foreign relations, as, for example, when the last treaty with France was subject to the ratification of the Canadian Parliament, when the German and Belgian Treaties were discussed, and when the question of International Copyright was brought up.

Then, so far as the United States are concerned, the ocean and inland fisheries are continually productive of disputed international points, as are the operations of the customs duties, and the bonding privileges along our vast conterminous frontiers ; the quarantining of cattle ; the use of the canals in the interior and the coasting laws, not to speak of the Behring Sea question. The laws for extradition of criminals between the two countries are worked out on both sides with the single object of suppressing crime.

There is one feature of the legislation of our neighbours which seems to Canadians to be harsh and barbarous, and which has resulted in an irresistible demand upon our Parliament for retaliation. For some years an Act of Congress has been in force known as the "Alien Labour Law," under the provisions of which no contract can be made with our citizens for employment in the United States under a penalty of a thousand dollars. In border towns American artisans were allowed to come across and compete with Canadian workmen with absolute freedom, while our people were and are as rigorously excluded by the American laws from employment there as if they were highway robbers. While regarding that law as a blot upon the legislation of the United States, the Canadian Parliament has been forced, simply as a measure of selfdefence, to resort to somewhat similar enactments against them. The relations between England and the United States are almost entirely dependent upon Canadian questions, which have to be dealt with, and practically settled, by the Canadian House of Commons. The peace of the Empire is thus often dependent upon the wisdom of the Colonial legislators.

Some thoughtful Englishmen believe the influence of Canada in that respect to be paramount. Mr. W. T. Stead, in addressing a Toronto audience not long ago used these words:

"Looking from the standpoint of London, it seems to us that the great question which lies before us as a race, is the question as to what are to be the future relations between the British Empire and the American Republic. . . . . This being the case, you can see how immensely important a position Canada holds in our outlook over the Universe. Canada is the pivot state, she holds the pass. It depends on you in Canada what these relations shall be. Your destiny, your manifest destiny, is to decide whether the British Empire and the American Republic are in the future to be friends or foes. . . . . The future of civilization and the hope of the world, depend upon the answer you will give. It is a great position which you hold. We, in our own country, may be as anxious to be friends with our American kinsfolk, as it is possible for mortals to be. We might even make it the great object of our state policy, but you could paralyze and render abortive anything we might attempt to do. You are the man on the horse in the present instance; we have to take the back seat. You are face to face with the actual questions, questions which arise and constantly will arise, which create friction between the two sections of the English speaking people. .... If I could speak so as to be heard by all your politicians and all your voters, I would implore you to remember that it lies with you to decide whether you will be the angel of peace, helping to unite into one the English speaking people, or whether you will be like another Cadmus sowing the dragon's teeth, from which will spring up armed men to desolate the world. This is the great question, which it is your destiny to decide."

If our position be such as Mr. Stead thinks it is, then our responsibilities are vast, and our powers for good or for evil are stupendous. Without going the length of this extract, we may be lead to believe that our intercourse with the United States should be friendly at all times, and that any displays of offensive colonial jingoism on our part would be both mischievous and undignified.

Even when purely domestic matters occupy the attention of the House of Commons their variety is remarkable. When a Canadian public man realizes the diversity of interests in his charge, and the vast territorial domain for which he legislates, his political vision must be broadened. To cure him of any notion that the House is only concerned in parish politics, he has but to listen to a general debate. The views of the extreme East of the Dominion may have just been expressed in vigorous French by the member whose constituents reside near the Straits of Belle Isle. The distance from Ottawa to those Straits is as great as the distance from London to the Straits of Messina. The next member to catch the Speaker's eye may represent the North-west of British Columbia on the Alaskan boundary. His constituents are as far from Ottawa as is Mecca from London; and the distance from Belle Isle through Ottawa to the boundary of Alaska is as great as from London to Northern China, or "Far Cathay."

The map of the United States at its widest part, from the point of Florida to the North-west of Washington State, will not scale as great a distance as from Ottawa to the extreme North-west of the Dominion.

No representative body was ever chosen

from so extended an area of the earth's surface to make laws for free electors.

While geographical importance in itself may be only a stimulus to vain-glory, yet the vast and varied natural resources that are spread from end to end of Canada have created a confidence in our national future, which no colony ever possessed before. All the foremost members of the Canadian Parliament, while they have due and loyal regard to their obligations as part of the Empire, are imbued with a full sense of their responsibility as builders of a great Northern Nation. They do not forget that the foundations now being laid by them must be broad and deep and sure, for on those foundations shall rest the national fabric of a Greater Britain.

The Leader of the House is always the First Minister, unless that office be held by a member of the Senate. Within the last six years two Premiers have sat in the Senate. Sir John Abbott was a Senator while his Cabinet held office after the death of Sir John

Macdonald, in 1891, and the Leader of the House of Commons at that time was Sir John Thompson, who succeeded to the premiership upon the death of Sir John Abbott.

Again, when Sir John Thompson died, one of his colleagues who sat in the Senate, Sir Mackenzie Bowell, became Premier, and the Ministerial Leader in the House of Commons was first Mr. George E. Foster, and then Sir Charles Tupper.

During all these changes the Leader of the Opposition party, both in and outside of the House, was the Hon. Wilfrid Laurier. When the general elections of the 23rd of June, 1896, placed him in power, the leadership of the Opposition fell to Sir Charles Tupper, who had been Premier at the time of the elections.

The position of leadership on either side cannot be held by a King Log. The Ministerial Leader is the commander-in-chief, who has not only to hold the forces of the enemy at bay, but must keep up the discipline in his own ranks. The mutiny of a small number of his followers would turn him out of power if they chose to cast their votes with the Opposition on almost any important measure of legislation.

The Leader of the Opposition is only second in importance in the House to the First Minister. He is alert by day and by night to press the governing party at all vulnerable points, and his followers must be kept in line to take advantage of all the mistakes of the adversary.

So great is the influence of the two leaders that many points relating to the conduct and order of business are settled between them, although the Ministerial Leader can always have his own way on essential matters if he insists upon the rights which his majority gives him, and which the rules of the House place in the hands of the Ministry.

For the conduct of the business of the House of Commons a code of rules has been adopted, largely based on those of the Imperial Parliament, but without the new rules of closure, which the English House has passed of late years. Among the Canadian rules it is indeed expressly enacted that in all unprovided cases the rules, usages and forms of the House of Commons of the United Kingdom of Great Britain and Ireland shall be followed. The procedure in the Canadian House is therefore harmonized, as far as possible, with the wisdom and experience of the Mother of Parliaments. The decisions of the great men who have presided over that assembly are carefully consulted to guide the Canadian Speakers, who thereby endeavour "to preserve the freedom and dignity of debate according to ancient usages."

In 1881, a section of the British House of Commons had detached itself from both of the regular parties of Ministerialists and Opposition, and entered upon an avowed course of obstruction. They brought matters to a crisis by holding the House in continuous sitting for forty-one hours, by sheer strength of lungs and physical endurance. This achievement was considered so unreasonable that, with the approval of the great majority on both sides of the Chamber, the Speaker arbitrarily put an end to the debate. The rules of closure were subsequently adopted to meet emergencies of a similar kind.

If Canada has no rules of closure it is not because she has had no long sittings in her House of Commons. In 1885, the Liberal Opposition were so much in earnest in opposing a Government measure relating to the Franchise, that they talked without pause and kept the House in continuous session for fifty-seven hours. But that was as nothing compared to the vigour and determination of those who, in 1896, were opposed to the Government's Remedial Bill relating to separate schools in Manitoba. The House went into Committee of the Whole on that Bill on a Monday afternoon at three o'clock. The discussion went on, scores of amendments were moved, and many of them were adopted, but when the committee rose at twelve o'clock on Saturday night, not one tenth part of the Bill had been gone through, and the sitting had lasted continuously for one hundred and twenty-nine hours! After the rest of Sunday, the same thing went on the next week for a seventy-five hours' sitting, when the Government withdrew the Bill. One broad distinction between the Canadian cases and the English one of 1881, is that in Canada about two-fifths of the members were strongly opposed to the measures of the Government, whereas in England only about one-tenth of the members were causing the obstruction. Without discussing the merits of the proceedings, the fact remains that the Canadian House of Commons has utterly excelled all the achievements of public assemblies in the history of the world, and has broken all records for endurance, if not for eloquence, in the parliamentary arena.

In the institutions of a new country it is always difficult to draw the line between decent observance of forms, and the excessive use of mere ceremony. This is particularly the case when that embodiment of democratic power—

the Canadian House of Commons—is modelled upon the historic Parliament of England, with its old traditions and the many forms which still cling around it.

It is also to be remembered that the head of our Executive is a Queen and Empress, who reigns over us, even if we govern ourselves; and that it is very difficult to see how the machinery of responsible parliamentary government could be carried on without a permanent head of that kind. Therefore, when the representative of our Queen comes down in state to the Senate, and desires to inform the faithful Commons of weighty matters, it is not at all surprising that he sends the Gentleman Usher of the Black Rod from the Senate to rap three times at the door of the Commons' Chamber, and, when admitted, to demand their attendance in the Upper House. Then the Commons itself has its Sergeant-at-Arms, who wears a sword, and carries the mace into the House before the Speaker, and, on adjournment, bears the "bauble" away again. The mace on the table shows that the House is in session, and it is but the outward symbol of the power of the people's representatives in Parliament assembled.

Did space permit, the description of an important debate in the House of Commons would give the best possible insight into the working of that Chamber. In the absence of that, the reader may make a nearer acquaintance with that body by perusing the pen pictures of several of its leaders which will be attempted in the next chapter.

CHAPTER IX.

THREE CANADIAN STATESMEN.

The Right Hon. Sir Wilfrid Laurier, G. C. M. G.—The Hon. Sir Charles Tupper, Bart., G. C. M. G.—The Hon. Sir Richard Cartwright, G. C. M. G.

Each elected representative body in the world presents features distinctive from those of any other. The American House of Representatives differs from the German House of Representatives, and the French Chamber of Deputies from the Italian Chamber of Deputies. An observer is not so much struck by the variance in powers, and rules, and forms, which exists, but by some intrinsic difference between the natures, and habits, and modes of thought of the separate assemblies.

The Canadian House of Commons is modelled so much upon its British prototype that one might easily believe that to know one was to know both. Far from that being the case, they differ widely. Each has an "atmosphere" of its own ; if one may say so, each has an "ear" of its own, and certainly a "voice." To be acclimatized and to breathe freely a member must have discovered and caught the "ear," otherwise the "voice" will inevitably and promptly pronounce his political doom.

While bright and speaking portraits of members of parliament have been sketched from the gallery, and from "behind the Speaker's chair," it is hard to find a precedent for any such sketches being given to the public by the actual occupant of the Speaker's chair.

The writer has weighed well the risk he incurs of criticism, in publishing an estimate of the public and parliamentary standing of a few of the leading members of the Canadian House of Commons. He has no thought of making harsh references to any of his fellow-members. They all, perhaps, receive their share of that treatment from one another.

It does not seem difficult to combine truth with impartiality in a friendly estimate of three

Right Hon. Sir Wilfrid Laurier, G.C.M.G.

leaders of the House, who are most in the public eye, and the writer will venture upon the not unpleasant task.

In the Canadian House of Commons there are three men who are its most striking figures, and the visitor to the gallery is always in hopes of seeing them and hearing them speak. They are Sir Wilfrid Laurier, Sir Charles Tupper and Sir Richard Cartwright.

SIR WILFRID LAURIER.

The Prime Minister, Sir Wilfrid Laurier, occupies the sixth seat in the front row, on the Speaker's right. That seat has been selected by every leader of the House of Commons, and the leader of the opposition sits on the other side just across the Clerk's table.

Sir Wilfrid has many personal advantages. He is tall, and graceful in his movements when speaking. His voice is clear and can be used to express the varied emotions in a speech with remarkable effect. In the House, unless when answering a remark made to him in

French, he always speaks in English, and an occasional touch of foreign accent is never enough to obscure his meaning, but lends a certain piquancy to his utterances.

The purity of his English is very noticeable, and may be partly accounted for from the fact that he acquired that language chiefly as a student, and from an industrious reading of the masters of the English tongue.

A young lawyer, with his head full of literature, he did what so many of that learned profession do in all countries, he first took to journalism and then drifted into politics. He was only thirty when he was elected to the Quebec Provincial Legislature. Even at that time he had made a name for himself as a lecturer on literary and political subjects, but chiefly in the language of his ancestors. To read his earliest public utterances is to discover in them the same elegance of diction, and the same breadth of view in treatment of Canadian affairs with which he delighted British audiences in the Jubilee year.

The larger sphere of Dominion politics soon attracted young Laurier, and at the age of thirty-three he gave up his seat in the Provincial legislature and was elected to the Canadian House of Commons. He was not a frequent speaker, but at once caught the ear of the House, and by a few carefully prepared speeches increased his already high reputation for eloquence.

When he came to Ottawa, the Liberal administration of Mr. Alex. Mackenzie was in power, and, a vacancy occurring in the French section of the Cabinet, Mr. Laurier was offered, and accepted, the position of Minister of Inland Revenue in 1877, after he had been but three years a member.

The Liberal Government was defeated in 1878, and Mr. Laurier sat in opposition continuously until July, 1896, when he became Premier of Canada.

Sir Wilfrid Laurier's position as Prime Minister is not a political accident or compromise. He was not a figure-head or stop-gap.

The chosen and tried leader of a great party in Opposition, he has simply continued to lead that party in power.

Mr. Laurier never made himself, to the same extent as did Bright, or Cobden, or Parnell, the champion of a single cause, or the advocate of a great reform, although it must be said that the grand idea of cementing the French and English races into a Canadian nation has been the burden of most of his political utterances, the aim of his highest ambition.

Always an advocate of religious and political liberty, the culmination of the dispute as to the Catholic Separate Schools of Manitoba, just before a general election, forced him to take a determined stand upon a question of first importance. On this he carried his own Catholic and French Province against much clerical interference, and commanded a decided majority in the House of Commons.

Sir Wilfrid is not what is known as merely a "safe" statesman. He is not afraid of his shadow. He goes out to face an enemy. He attacks an injustice or a wrong fearlessly. This he did in opposition. It is proved already that in power he is not afraid to move onwards. Large schemes have no terrors for him when his judgment approves of them. He is not an opportunist. He is a man of progressive action. There will be no stagnation in his policy.

He possesses a certain natural graciousness of disposition, and those genial and sympathetic qualities which win hearts, and make life pleasanter than it would otherwise be. He is easily the most popular man in the House, and has been so for many years.

His literary studies have enlarged and illustrated his statesmanship, and have enriched his oratory. A cultivated historic sense gives a distinctive breadth to all his speeches.

Lord Beaconsfield made a charge against English Liberalism that it was in its essence cosmopolitan while Conservatism was national. This cannot be said of Sir Wilfrid Laurier's Liberalism. He has devoted his life to the creation of a united Canadian nationality by the political fusion of the French and English races. Nor is he cosmopolitan in his patriotism, unless the Imperial idea, which is so attractive to him, can be considered as derogatory to Canadian nationality. To the minds of many, the loftiest conception of Canadian nationality is that our country should become one of a vast federation of free British nations, paramount in power, in wealth and in greatness.

SIR CHARLES TUPPER.

Canada, in the year of grace 1897, has still a group of public men whose services in connection with the founding of the Dominion entitle them to be called the "Fathers of Confederation." This title is awarded to all delegates who took part in the conferences at Charlottetown, Quebec and London between 1864, and the passage of the British North America Act of 1867, which created the Federal Union of the Dominion of Canada.

But one of this venerable group holds a seat in the House of Commons in the Parliament of

Hon. Sir Charles Tupper, Bart., G.C.M.G.

1896, and he is Sir Charles Tupper, Bart., leader of Her Majesty's loyal Opposition.

As Prime Minister of his Province of Nova Scotia, in 1864, Sir Charles warmly espoused the cause of a Federal Union. He carried that measure through the Provincial Legislature, although there was an active agitation against it among many, who claimed that a question of such vital importance should be submitted to the verdict of the electors. The strength of this feeling was made manifest at the first Federal elections, when the "antis" swept the Province. Time, however, has largely softened the hostility of Nova Scotia to confederation, although many of the people of that Province still protest against the manner of carrying it.

No other Canadian of to-day has had so long and varied a public career as Sir Charles Tupper, nor has held so many distinguished offices. He entered the Nova Scotia Legislature in 1855, where he soon became a member of the Government and Prime Minister. After Confederation he was not long in reaching the

Federal Cabinet, from which he retired to fill the office of High Commissioner to London. Returning to Canada he was chosen leader of the House of Commons in Sir Mackenzie Bowell's Cabinet, and on 27th April, 1896, he became for a short time Prime Minister of Canada, until the defeat of his party at the general elections of June.

His predominant characteristics are boldness in statement, and energy in action. No obstacles appall him, no combination of difficulties can daunt him. Among the earliest, as well as the latest events of his political life, this trait is displayed. In bringing Nova Scotia into the Union, a third of a century ago, he undertook a herculean task, which he accomplished. In 1896, when he sought to carry out Federal Remedial Legislation to override the Provincial legislation of Manitoba relating to Separate Schools, he entered upon a task beyond his powers, but he fell with his face to the foe.

The position of High Commissioner in London is understood to have been very much to his taste. Yet on more than one occasion he risked that position, and left its dignified ease, to plunge into the turmoil of a general election in Canada at the call of his party.

Upon his return to the House of Commons in 1896, some of his friends feared that a leader with the burden of seventy-five years to carry might be scarcely equal physically to sustain the heavy fighting required of him. His indomitable pluck, however, seemed to call out latent energies within his frame, and he stood the longest sittings on record in any deliberative body, and a continuous and bitter struggle in Committee, without apparent fatigue.

His oratory is forcible in the House, and most effective upon the platform. With a voice of great power, and with an impassioned manner, he is capable of unlimited denunciation of a policy which he condemns.

It must be said that he does not necessarily condemn a measure simply because it forms part of the policy of his opponents. On the contrary, he has a courage, often rare in public men, which enables him on occasion to rise above party fault-finding and to give the Government credit for some of their measures which he believes to be in the public interest.

He is jealous of the honour of the House, and does much by his example in supporting the rulings of the Speaker to maintain its order and dignity.

His important position as leader of the Opposition enables him to co-operate with the Government in facilitating the public business; and he is most punctilious in carrying out the spirit of all understandings arrived at across the House.

SIR RICHARD CARTWRIGHT.

Beside the Prime Minister sits his Minister of Trade and Commerce, Sir Richard Cartwright. Although Sir Richard is to-day a stout Liberal, and has been so for over a quarter of a century, he entered public life, in 1863, as a "stern and unbending Tory." Like Gladstone, however, he has traversed the long

Hon. Sir Richard Cartwright, G.C.M.G.

distance from Toryism to Liberalism by a steady intellectual movement, which one political party would characterize as backsliding, the other as progress. A political pupil of Sir Alan McNab, a former Canadian Premier, he resented the methods which he believed Sir John Macdonald employed to secure the leadership of the Conservative party. The breach widened till, at the general election of 1872, he had fully detached himself from the party led by Sir John Macdonald, and naturally accepted office in the Liberal Administration of Mr. Alex. Mackenzie in 1873.

He was a young member of the Canadian Legislature, when the sharp struggles took place which brought about the Confederation of the British North American Colonies. He was too new to public life to become a member of the Conferences which evolved the Federal Constitution, but he gave the scheme his hearty support.

His features are strong and marked, and indicate the directness and vigour of his disposition. Had he been a military chief, his countenance and bearing would have inspired his followers with confidence that he could always be depended upon to lead them to an aggressive campaign. So it has been in his political warfare. In his long years of opposition, from 1878 to 1896, he gave and received hard blows. He seldom waited for an attack, but preferred the offensive, and carried the war into Africa by his fierce assaults upon the Conservative trade policy and administrative acts.

No living Canadian has made a more profound study than Sir Richard of the economical conditions of the Dominion, and his speeches in criticism of the Budgets of many years are models of clear and condensed financial exposition.

He is a voracious reader of books, and his varied and accurate knowledge of English literature must have been acquired by unceasing study of the best authors ever since his student days at Trinity College, Dublin.

It is often a literary treat to listen to his

speeches. His invective is powerful and his sarcasm scathing, but always clothed in the choicest language, with a flavour of the classic rather than the modern English style.

This consummate political gladiator at times lays aside his sword and shield. When leading the House, in the absence of the First Minister, he can display a most courteous and winning manner, and in that rôle is ever ready with the soft answer that turneth away wrath.

CHAPTER X.

VICE-REGAL FUNCTIONS.

Governor-General as Political Head——Acts on Advice of his Ministers——Executive Acts——Opening and Prorogueing Parliament——Social Head——Her Excellency's Influence——Drawing Rooms——Manner of Presentation——Government House——State Dinners——Parliamentary Dinners——Highland Pipers——American Visitors——Balls——Historical Ball of 1896——Garden Parties——Skating and Tobogganing Parties——Bon-fire——Ski-löbning——Good Influence of Lord and Lady Aberdeen.

The Governor-General of Canada has a two-fold responsibility. He is the political head, under whom Canada governs herself; and he is the social head, under whose lead and example Canada tries to enjoy herself. As representative of the Queen he calls to his councils a Prime Minister and Cabinet who must possess the confidence and control of the House of Commons. Under his Ministers' advice he makes appointments in Her Majesty's

THE EARL OF ABERDEEN,
GOVERNOR-GENERAL OF CANADA.

name to offices high and low, from Lieutenant-Governors and Judges to landing-waiters. He approves of orders-in-council, and, under the same advice, performs all executive acts of government required of him. In the Queen's name he assents to all Bills passed by the Senate and House of Commons. He goes to the Senate Chamber arrayed in a brilliant uniform, and driven in a dashing four-in-hand coach with liveried postilions, and surrounded by a troop of cavalry, to open or to prorogue Parliament. A battery fires a salute in his honour, and everything is done in as impressive a manner as possible.

In his political aspect the Governor-General stands alone, for is he not the august representative of Majesty itself? In his social aspect, however, the lady by his side shares a divided honour and responsibility with him. Their Excellencies usually give a drawing-room in the Senate Chamber on the night of the first Saturday after the opening of Parliament. They are supported by a brilliant staff, consisting of the A.D.C.'s and a score or two of officers of the different volunteer corps in Ottawa. Full dress is, of course, *de rigueur*. There are often many hundreds presented, and to the *debutante* it is a trying ceremony. Each person must be provided with two cards, one of which is left with a member of the staff within the entrance to the Chamber. From that point each walks through a lane of officers, and as the Throne is approached on which their Excellencies stand, the other card is given to one of the A.D.C.'s, who passes it to another, who awaits the proper time, and then calls out the name in a distinct voice. Then the man bows, or the lady curtseys low, first to the Governor-General, and next, with a sidelong move, to Her Excellency. After the presentation, those who have made their obeisances may pass behind the rows of officers who line the way from the entrance, and, standing on the elevated sides of the floor, may watch the victims approaching the ordeal, and criticise their appearance, dress and curtseys.

Senate Interior, Ottawa.

It must not be supposed that all are admitted as they happen to arrive. The high dignitaries, who outrank the Senators according to the Table of Precedence for Canada, are the first to be presented with their wives and daughters; then come Senators, then members of the Commons, and afterwards the rest of the world and his wife and daughters. When the reception is over their Excellencies and other invited guests pay short visits and have a cup of tea in the apartments of the Speakers of the Senate, and of the House of Commons.

Government House, or the official residence of the Governor-General, is a large, rambling mass of buildings named Rideau Hall. It stands among its gardens and prettily-wooded grounds, about two miles down the river from the Houses of Parliament, and from its terraces the national buildings are outlined against the western sky. Its public apartments, ballroom and reception rooms are sufficiently large, and the rest of it is more homelike than stately.

An annual official function is the State

dinner that is given at the opening of the session. The guests are the high political and other dignitaries, and the permanent heads of departments. Then there are a series of Parliamentary dinners, at which it is expected that members of both Houses and their wives and daughters will have an opportunity of meeting their Excellencies. A feature of such dinners that is a novel one, is the introduction, before the ladies leave the dining room, of one or two braw Highland pipers, resplendent in kilts, and wearing the tartan of their chieftain, John Gordon, Earl of Aberdeen. These gallant fellows march several times round the table, and finally take up their stand behind the Governor-General, all the while playing, with a zeal and vigour that does them the highest credit, a full collection of warlike pibrochs and gay strathspeys. The effect is excellent, and the guests feel that they are welcomed at the feast of a real Highland chieftain, by a custom that his ancestors had observed far back in the older days of Scottish history.

Government House, Ottawa.—National Buildings in the Distance.

During the month of February, 1898, a special train arrived in Ottawa, bearing a distinguished party of Americans on a flying visit to the Canadian Capital. Their Excellencies were able to invite them to a skating party in the afternoon, and a dinner in the evening. When the stately piper marched down the dining hall in kilt and tartan, with ribands flying from the pipes, it was noticed that the air he played was not a reel or strathspey of his native land. Gradually, pleased smiles broke over the faces of the visitors when they recognized that their thoughtful host had caused them to be welcomed to his hospitable roof by the inspiriting notes of "Marching through Georgia."

Rideau Hall lights up well, and its interior is at its best on the occasion of one of the large balls which their Excellencies often give. No residents in Ottawa can expect an invitation unless they have taken the trouble to put down their names in the visitors' book at Government House, although it must not be inferred that no scrutiny is made of the names on the book.

A most memorable and unique historical ball was given by their Excellencies in the Senate Chamber in 1896. Different epochs of Canadian history were represented, and prominent ladies had each charge of a "Court," in which the costumes and dances were arranged to represent distinct periods.

When the weather smiles of a summer afternoon, the garden parties at Government House are always enjoyable. On one occasion Her Excellency told the ladies, who were invited, to bring the children; and the little ones were delighted by a performing troupe of dogs and ponies, who had been playing at a theatre in town, and were thoughtfully engaged for the entertainment of the juveniles at the garden party.

Winter's ice and snow lend an opportunity to Government House to afford their guests a singularly beautiful spectacle. A card for an evening skating party is the modest form of invitation; but what a scene of enchantment does that bring one to! Close to the house is a rather deep ravine or hollow with an open glade between evergreen trees. In the upper part, and nearest the house, are skating and curling rinks, and a band encourages the skaters to break into a waltz. Upon the surface of the snow in an open space a huge bonfire is blazing and making the scene as light as day. In the recesses of the woods a glow of Chinese lanterns lights up another skating rink. Built high up above the slopes of the ravine are the dizzy slides through whose icy troughs the laden toboggans shoot with the speed of an avalanche, and are sent flying through the level snow far adown the glade.

The skilöber is also to be seen taking headlong slides down hills, and making extraordinarily fast time anywhere on the hard surface of the snow.

It is impossible to refer to the present occupants of Government House without a word to indicate the thought that is uppermost in the minds of all who have come in contact with them. What Lord and Lady Aberdeen seem to be most remarkable for is their intense earnestness and desire to accomplish good for Canada and her people. Her Excellency has not the same opportunity for making speeches and addresses as her husband, but she seeks out, all the more, other ways in which she can interest and help her fellow women to improve and elevate their lives. Their kindly zeal permeates the land, their good influence cannot be transient, and, after they leave us, their memory will live long in the hearts of the Canadian people.

CHAPTER XI.

WINTER SPORTS AT OTTAWA.

Perfection of Canadian Winter Sports——Ottawa, Montreal, Quebec——Ice-Boating on Toronto Bay——Three Months Hard Winter——Canadians Freeze in English Winters——A Winter Night——Sleighs and Furs——Sleigh-bells——Snow-Shoes and Ski——A Show-Shoeing Party——Skating——Governor-General on Ice——Night Scene in Rink——Dances on Skates——The Game of Hockey——Curling a Great Canadian Game——The Vice-Regal Rink——Tobogganing——The Indian Sledge——Going Down a Slide——Its Terrors——Its Delights——A Duffer's Mischances——Girls in a Snow Drift.

After all, what country in the world can approach Canada in the attraction of its winter sports? In Ottawa, Montreal and Quebec is to be found the perfection of winter life. The ice-boating on Toronto Bay is probably the best to be found anywhere, owing to the number of times during the winter that fresh ice is formed, either by a clean sheet of new ice, or by a sharp frost after the flooding of the surface snow in a thaw. At Ottawa there are three months to be depended upon, every winter, for good hard weather and snow, beginning in December and ending in March. Even if the thermometer runs down to zero and below, everyone is prepared for it, both indoors and out of doors ; and Canadians who spend a winter in England always wish themselves at home again in order to be reasonably warm. What if the air is sharp and stings a bit? Is it not more than exhilarating, almost intoxicating in its glorious, clear, dry crispness? If the Canadian winter is new to you, and if the brightness of high noon upon the snows is too dazzling for your unaccustomed eyes, save those eyes for the softened splendours of the moonlight, or the still glories of a starry night, lit up with flashes of the aurora, that hangs its tinted banners athwart the Northern sky.

Time cannot press heavily upon old or young in an Ottawa winter. Out of doors the frost and snow furnish sleigh driving, and snowshoeing, skating and curling, hockey, ski-löbning and tobogganing. The cab or coupé of summer is laid up in its winter quarters, and in its place a graceful and comfortable sleigh is brought out. The season is long enough to warrant cabby in spending a round sum in fur robes. His favourite is the long-haired skin of the brown musk-ox, and when one of these swings gracefully over the back, another covers the high seat upon which the driver is perched, and a third is spread upon the knees of the "fares," the sleigh looks well equipped, and the effect is decidedly good. The driver is protected by fur cap and mitts, and by a coat of the skin of the Canadian coon, or the dog of Astrakhan. The passengers who are men probably wear Persian lamb, and the gentle sex, here, as elsewhere, delight in sealskin, of course, although for most men, and many women, it is becoming the correct thing at Ottawa to wear the warm, cheap, serviceable coon-skin coat.

The municipal ordinances in Canada demand that every sleigh shall have bells. This is not an æsthetic, but an utilitarian, requirement, in order to prevent collisions, as there is no rattling of wheels to give warning, but the sledges pass silently over the smooth surface of the frozen snow.

What wonder that Poe gives second place among all his bells to

> "The sledges with the bells—
> Silver bells!
> What a world of merriment their melody
> foretells!"

The cross-country tramp need scarcely be abandoned for a day in the neighbourhood of Ottawa. In fact, the frost renders even pond and swamp, lake and river, "walkable" in winter, and with the snowshoes of the Indian, or the ski of the Scandinavian, much new country may be investigated in an afternoon's stroll. While snowshoeing has always been familiar to the residents of the Ottawa Valley, whose pleasure or business has taken them off the beaten track, the use of the ski, or skilöbning, has only been recently introduced by the occupants of Government House, and has become so popular that the ski are now made in the town. They are long, narrow strips of tough wood, generally of soft maple, from three to four inches in breadth, and from six to eight feet in length, an inch or an inch and a half thick in the middle, but thinner towards the ends, and slightly curved up in the front. One is secured on each foot in such a way as to be easily cast off in case of accident. On level, or ascending ground the skilöber can propel himself with a sharp-pointed stick, but the highest enjoyment is when, standing on his ski, he rushes down a hill with the speed of a hurricane.

The Canadian snowshoe, with its light frame woven with deerskin thongs, and its graceful shape, is a familiar object. Snowshoers of both sexes delight to array themselves in blanket coats and sashes of many colours. Away they march over snow-drifts and fences, or down the frozen river, with a sense of freedom to trespass on any man's land, or water, that is not given to mortals under any other known conditions.

To claim skating as a Canadian invention would scarcely be safe, in case these lines should be read "abroad" (meaning outside of the Dominion). Yet no one could successfully deny that this "poetry of motion" is more loved and practised in Canada than in any other country. The climate has placed it within our reach, our tastes have made it one of the national pastimes. From the Rocky Mountains to the Gulf of St. Lawrence every Canadian boy and girl, of six years of age and upwards, is excited by the first sign of frost. The waters of every rink and pond are watched by eager eyes. The skates are looked up, and poor Papa is soon made to understand how many little feet have outgrown last year's skates. At Ottawa each Governor-General has always felt it a pleasant duty to show his zeal for skating by steady practice at his own well-kept rinks. There are in the town enough rinks to meet the demand of skaters while the frost lasts. Nothing can be prettier than a night scene in a large, covered rink, when it is well filled with graceful girls in their swagger ice costumes, and well set up young men in their skating jackets. It is band night, and the music seems to give all the skaters a certain harmony of motion. At last the "lancers" is played, and partners are sought. Only skilled performers can take part in this dance, yet it is surprising how many go through its mazes with success. Then, next, a waltz is struck up, and it seems as if it were composed for the graceful swing of the skating couples, who slide and glide with every undulation of the music.

While skating is an art it is not a game. Yet it is a foundation for a splendid game that is only played in perfection upon Canadian rinks. When the frost and snow have driven the football teams off the field, the players can keep in training by joining a "hockey" club. The game is played by seven on each side, and the hockey sticks bear some resemblance to the old inverted walking sticks that were used for shinny. Instead of a ball, a rubber puck, or disc, is driven or lifted by a shoving motion, which is not a blow. The puck is sufficiently elastic to carom from the wooden sides of the rinks. The players on each side are : a goal-keeper, point, cover point and four forwards. The goals won are the only points scored in a match, which lasts for an hour of play, with thirty minutes for each half. The off-side rule is practically the same as in football. Ottawa has several hockey teams.

The Scottish race is too influential in Canada not to have left its mark in every walk of life, and its national game of curling was introduced in our earliest days. If the seed cannot be said to have been sown in a fertile soil, the "stanes" have been placed in the hands of "braw chiels." The village mill-pond is cleared of snow for the friendly contest, when

"The curling stane
Slides murmuring o'er the icy plain."

In towns, the solid men, who have built the skating rinks for the youngsters, are care-

Vice-Regal Curling Rink—Lord Dufferin's Time.

ful to lay out beneath a sheltering roof one or more curling rinks, where matches and bonspiels are played with immense spirit, and much satisfaction to all parties. An adjournment usually takes place to a hospitable board, groaning under the curler's fare of "beef and greens," and more or less fluid concomitants. In Ottawa curling the Vice Regal rink can hold its own with the best of them.

The toboggan, like the snowshoe, is a product of the Red Indians' untutored mind. He knew enough to keep himself on the surface of the deepest snow by the one, and his provisions, papooses and general impedimenta were floated along behind him on the other. Some unerring instinct must have taught him to fashion out of the materials at his hand utensils for his winter life, as perfect and as useful in their way as the beaver's hut, or the oriole's nest. What was good enough for papooses is good enough for the enjoyment of full-grown Canadians in their long winters. The toboggan is formed of flat hardwood boards a quarter of an inch in thickness. Its average width is eighteen inches, and length eight feet. The bow is turned up and back so as to throw off loose snow. Along the edges run strong, light rods which serve as handles and as stays, to which cross-pieces are bound to hold the boards together. The under side is polished to the highest degree of smoothness, and the upper side is comfortably padded. Stout thongs made fast to the top of the curved bow are used to draw it, and sometimes to guide it. Any snow-clad hill serves for the sport, if there is a long level at its foot clear of obstructions, over which the toboggan can career after its plunge down the steep slope. The perfection of tobogganing is found on the artificial slides which are raised to a dizzy height, with a wide, deep trough, coated with snow and ice, pitching towards the ground at a fearful angle. As the foot is approached the slope becomes more gentle until it is worked off to the level that stretches for perhaps half a mile beyond. Wooden steps are built up to

TOBOGGANING NEAR OTTAWA.

the platform at the top of the slide where the start is made. The tobogganing dress is much the same as that worn by snowshoers. Fur cap, or red or blue toque, blanket coat, and sash, warm mittens and buckskin moccasins. The toboggan is good for one passenger, better for two, and best for three, as the momentum of a heavy load carries it fast and far. The post of danger and delight is, of course, the front seat, and this is always given to a lady, because a man must be at the back to steer with hands or foot. It is not every girl who will trust herself for the first time to the slide, but after persuasion from her escort and assuring words from older hands, she is carefully tucked in, and, grasping the rods at each side, off they go before she can change her mind. Death, certain and sudden, seems before her! She shuts her eyes, her breath is gone, the keen air stings, the snow-drift smites her cheeks like hail, the whirlwind roars about her, and the rush of the toboggan over ice and snow shrieks like the scream of a rocket. Now is the time to form good resolutions; but when four or five hundred feet are passed over in one second, the terrifying conditions soon change, the noise becomes less, the wind is not so cutting, and the sense of dropping through the air has ceased. The novice ventures to open her eyes, and to draw her breath. Why, how "perfectly lovely" it all is now! Shooting along on the level snow, past the firs bending under the weight of their winter mantle, among the laughing groups, returning to climb the stairs again, all the terror of a moment ago is forgotten in the sense of safety and triumph. Will she take another turn? Of course she will, and still another, and always another, until the party breaks up, or a cruel chaperone tears her away.

It is true that sometimes a duffer is steering. While the highest speed is on, he fortunately can scarcely divert the toboggan from the trough, but when the level is reached, it is quite within his power, by misdirected efforts to swing it to one side, and upset the passengers, sending them rolling over and over in the snow. This performance may be a trifle undignified, but it is seldom dangerous. Canadian girls, by some mysterious combination of garments, seem to be quite at home even when sitting in a snow-drift with the thermometer at zero.

CHAPTER XII.

OTTAWA SUMMER SPORTS.

Maple sugar picnics—Cricket—Legislators play—Polo—Golf—Legislators again—Mr. Arthur Balfour on Golf—Tennis—Lacrosse—Indians no longer Champions—Athletic Club—Canoeing—In the Woods—Longfellow's lines—French Voyageurs' Canoe Song—Canoe Club in Ottawa—Ladies expert paddlers—Rowing Club—Football—Ottawa College Rugby Champions—Physical culture in Canada—Fishing Clubs—Lake fishing for trout and bass—Among the Laurentian Hills—Size of trout—Specimen catch—Excellent Flavour—Anecdote—Maskinonge—Lake trout—Small game—Duck—Partridge, or Ruffed Grouse—Woodcock—Snipe—Plover—Rideau Rifle Ranges—Red deer hunting—Pot hunting prohibited—Still-hunting and stalking—As wolves decrease deer multiply—Moose—Algonquin Park—Immense area—Strictly preserved for protection of fish, game and fur—Nature of country—Well wooded and watered—The forest primeval—Beaver returning—Story of a cow moose and calves—A she bear—Wolves.

While the ice and snows are disappearing, and "Winter lingers in the lap of Spring," there is a short period when out-of-door sports are at a standstill. It is true this is the time when the maple sugar is being made, and

LOVERS' WALK, ON PARLIAMENT HILL.

picnics are often given to pay a visit to some maple groves in the neighbourhood, and to make toffy by pouring the hot syrup upon the snow, and to eat the fresh sugar round the camp fire where the big kettles of sap have been boiling night and day.

Ottawa is well provided with clubs for summer sport. Cricket is played on a capital ground adjoining Rideau Hall, and some Ottawa players are always chosen on the team representing Canada in the international matches with the United States. During the summer sessions of Parliament that are often held, the wickets are pitched on the lawn in front of the Buildings, and the legislators of both Houses wield the willow with great effect.

There are not many Polo clubs in Canada, but there is one in the capital, where it is found that ponies from the North-west prairies, called bronchos, form excellent mounts.

The Golf Club is flourishing, and it is a treat to play over their breezy links beyond the river. The hazards are all that could be desired, and the turf is admirable. The links are perhaps the best in Canada, except those at Quebec, and some good players are to be seen any fine afternoon in their bright red club coats making their drives, approaches and putts, and occasionally struggling with the bunkers.

The hospitality of the club is liberally extended to golf-players among the non-resident legislators. It is one of their greatest treats to go round the links on a holiday or in the morning before the House meets. We believe with Arthur J. Balfour, golfer and statesman, that "a tolerable day, a tolerable green, and a tolerable opponent, supply, or ought to supply, all that any reasonably constituted being should require in the way of entertainment. Care may sit beside the horseman; she never presumes to walk with the caddie."

The ladies of Ottawa are particularly strong in Tennis, and the Ladies' Provincial Championship is sometimes worthily held by one of them.

The game of Lacrosse is another debt which Canadians owe to the Indians, and for many years the savage teams were invincible. When the whites took it up, some thirty years ago, they had only learnt it as men. Since then the small boys have been busy at it, and have grown up to it as the English have to Cricket. The result is that no Indian teams can face a white one now, nor can any foreign team play at all an equal game with a first-class Canadian one. The Ottawa lacrosse teams are amongst the best in Canada, and visitors to the capital are always highly delighted to witness a first-class match. In no other game is the skill of the player in the field so apparent to the spectator, and in none are the varying chances so exciting.

Canoeing is another Canadian sport which is borrowed from the Indians, whose birch-bark canoes are the most graceful and useful of water-craft. In fishing trips where there are long land portages to be made from lake to lake, or in order to pass falls or strong rapids, the vessel that carries the sportsman must in turn be carried by him on his shoulders over rocks and hills and through the woods. It is nothing to whip up a light birch-bark canoe, turn it upside down and balance it with a paddle stretched between the thwarts resting on each shoulder, and carry it a mile at a stretch. Other members of the party are "packing" or carrying the provisions, blankets, etc., across the portage on their backs, and the canoe is slipped into the water to be ready for loading when the freight arrives. What can be more graceful or picturesque than the little craft as she floats there with a draft of only two or three inches! Longfellow does not say a word too much when he tells us :—

>"And the forest's life was in it,
>All its mystery and its magic,
>All the lightness of the birch tree,
>All the toughness of the cedar,
>All the larch's supple sinews;
>And it floated on the river
>Like a yellow leaf in Autumn,
>Like a yellow water lily."

What the camel is to the desert the birch-bark canoe is to the Canadian forest and stream. In all the northern country it is the great means of locomotion for sportsmen, fur traders or gold-hunters, before roads or railways come.

The cheerful voices of the voyageurs may be often heard echoing through the gloomy pine forests, the measured dip of their paddles keeping time with the rhythmical cadence of their favourite canoe song, "*En Roulant ma Boule Roulant.*"

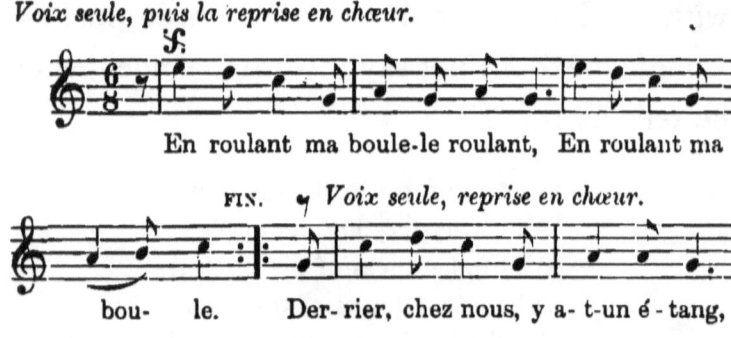

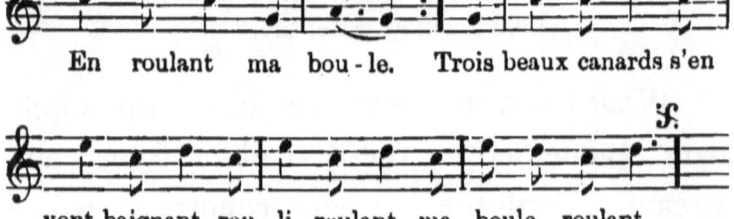

The air is a very catchy one, and a verse and the chorus are given above in the vernacular with the music.

Ottawa has a large canoe club at the pretty suburb of Rockcliffe, a mile or so down the river, where there are nearly a hundred canoes. They are mostly cedar canoes of Rice Lake or Peterboro' make, as the birch-bark are not so suitable for sailing. Excursions down the river with afternoon tea, made on the shore, are favorite uses for the fleet. With a portage up the locks the canoes can be launched in the upper reaches of the canal, and a delightful paddle can be had among woods and fields along its banks. No canoe is considered to be properly trimmed unless there is a lady on board, and Ottawa girls are always able and willing to work their passage on a short canoe trip.

The Ottawa Rowing Club, with boathouses at the foot of the locks, is an old-established and flourishing institution. They have all description of craft from racing shells to family boats, and have turned out some excellent crews at the regattas that are held every summer on so many Canadian and American waters. The Club has a number of canoes as well as boats.

Of course on both the river and the canal there are numbers of private boat-houses, and also plenty of boats for hire.

Football has brought athletic honours to Ottawa for many years. There is a good club among the townspeople, but Ottawa College can boast of a Rugby team that is easily the champion of Canada. Not only every college team, but every other Rugby team in the country have often had to lower their colours before this all-conquering fifteen. They contend that if they could arrange for a match with the American College Rugby champions they would achieve for us a national victory. It is quite possible they would, but the whole system of play in the United States is so different from either English or Canadian Rugby, that it is scarcely to be hoped that such a meeting can be brought about.

There are two good and prospering athletic clubs in Ottawa, and no considerable Canadian city can be found which is without one or more. A hopeful and healthful taste among the youth for physical exercises is a characteristic feature of Canadian life. Without degenerating into brute force it gives a manly tone to the people, which can never come from mere culture of the intellect. There is no fear of brain culture being neglected in Canada, where the system of education from the primary schools to the universities is as good as in any country. It is an excellent sign that the good sense of the people gives fair play to muscle and physical culture.

Across the river the Laurentian Hills are full of lakes innumerable, of all shapes and sizes, which in their turn are full of trout of all sizes. There are a few where black bass abound, but *salmo fontinalis* cannot thrive with that voracious fish for neighbour, and in a lake where bass are plentiful there are none but the very largest speckled trout, which have run down from brooks tributary to the lake. In all the other lakes there are speckled red trout, and in many, with them, are the larger grey trout. Practically all of these lakes have been leased from the Quebec Government by fishing clubs in Ottawa, who are very hospitable to strangers, and no visitor with letters need ever miss a few days of the best of fishing, if he chooses to ask for it. Each club secures several lakes lying near together, and some have as many as a dozen. The lakes run from twenty or thirty acres up to 200 or 300 acres, or more, in extent. There is very little settlement near these waters, which lie among beautifully wooded hills, and one guardian can look after a number of lakes. There is generally a snug club house in some central position from which all the lakes belonging to it can be reached. Plenty of boats are provided on each lake for members of the club, and they are necessary, because it is difficult in most places to make a cast from the heavily wooded shores. May and September are the months for this fishing, as the mosquitoes become very ravenous in June, and in July and August the trout do not rise at all freely. In the latter part of May a visit to one of these preserves is delightful. The trees are bursting into leaf and blossom. The woods are full of trailing arbutus, witch hazel, trilliums, and a score of other bright-hued flowers. The loud drum of the Canadian partridge, or ruffed grouse, is echoing through the forest, and the throat of every bird is vocal if he has any music in his soul. The temperature allures one to spend the whole livelong day upon the water, and in yielding to that temptation, the chances are ten to one that a heavy basket of trout will be the reward of virtue.

The size of the fish varies very much in different lakes. A small stream of a few hundred yards in length may connect a couple of lakes, and in one the trout will be small and numerous, in the other of quite a larger class, but much more scarce. At one of the best lakes two men were fishing two days in the month of September, 1896; they took in that time with the fly 123 speckled trout, and the catch weighed 182 pounds. That was an exceedingly good record for these lakes, and cannot be easily beaten anywhere.

The writer has killed trout in many waters from the Province of Quebec to British Columbia, and knows of no trout equal in flavour to those of the Ottawa lakes. A distinguished Canadian statesman from one of the Maritime Provinces had often asserted that no fresh water fish in the country were fit to eat. Having been fortunate enough to bring back a fine basket of trout from one of these lakes the writer invited the legislator to breakfast and helped him to some of the fish. "Well," said he, "I don't know where you got this fish and I won't say I haven't tasted as good, but I will say I never tasted better." Which was a signal triumph for the poor fresh water fish

Up the Ottawa River there is good bass fishing in the frequent rapids, and many trout streams flow into it on both sides. A few hours on the rail, by either the Gatineau Valley

Railway or the Pontiac on the Quebec side, or by the Canadian Pacific or Parry Sound Railways on the Ontario side, will take the fisherman to numerous streams and lakes well stocked with maskinonge and bass, or with red and grey trout. The latter, like the maskinonge, are taken with a trolling line and spinner of some kind, and both maskinonge and grey, or lake, trout will sometimes turn the scale at fifteen or twenty or even thirty pounds apiece.

Small game is fairly plentiful near Ottawa. An enterprising club acquired a quantity of marsh bogs and islands some twenty miles down the river, which they have sown with wild rice, the favourite food of the wild duck. The result is that on their own preserves and for a long distance down the stream, the rice has thriven and spread, and attracted large quantities of duck.

The woods near Ottawa are full of partridge, as we call the ruffed grouse; in the covers along the margin of streams a few woodcock are to be picked up, snipe in the marshes and golden plover in the fields. No very large bags can be made near the town, but a hard-working sportsman and good shot can get several brace in the day's tramp.

For those who desire rifle practice the Rideau Range is at their service. It is prettily situated on the banks of the river from which it is named, and is used for the matches of the Dominion Rifle Association, as well as for the competition of the local corps of volunteers.

In the autumn scores of hunters look for more interesting game than the targets at the range. In the short season of fifteen days, from the first to the fifteenth of November, it is wonderful how many red deer are killed in Ontario. The railways running west up the Ottawa River soon bring one to the happy hunting grounds. The former pot-hunting practice of running the deer into lakes with dogs and shooting them from a canoe, has been stopped by law. The hunter now watches his chance for a shot on a runway, or still-hunts and stalks the deer among the rocks and trees.

The great enemy of the red deer is the wolf. As the back country is opened up by settlers and railways, the wolves are frightened away and the deer multiply greatly. In the woods of the Upper Ottawa there are still a number of moose, who are increasing rapidly owing to their protection by a strict close season that has been established for some years. That noble game is said to have become plentiful under the protection of the rangers in Algonquin Park.

This Park is a wise creation of the Ontario Provincial Government. Out of their public domain in the wild, and agriculturally unpromising areas on the watershed between the Upper Ottawa and the Georgian Bay, they have set apart and withdrawn from sale or settlement, a block which contains 1,733 square miles, of which 181 are covered by water. The Act for the establishment of the Park was passed in 1893, and is distinct enough in the following statement of its purpose: "The said tract of land is hereby reserved and set apart as a public park and forest reservation, fish and game preserve, health resort and pleasure ground, for the benefit, advantage, and enjoyment of the people of the Province." It is all placed under the control of a superintendent, wardens and rangers, among whose duties are " The preservation and protection of game and fish, of wild birds generally, and of any and all animals in the park, and the destruction of wolves, bears and other noxious or injurious or destructive animals." Shooting and fishing can only be done under special license, and no pot hunting is permitted. The setting apart of this large tract for pleasure and sport has received the hearty approval of the people, and the officials are well supported in their efforts to make it a special paradise for sportsmen and campers.

The Park consists of undulating and rocky land, interspersed with streams and innumerable lakes abounding in fish. The forest spreads in an almost unbroken expanse over the whole tract, and although equally magnificent cover for game may have been preserved before for royal sportsmen, it has never been preserved elsewhere for the "benefit, advantage and enjoyment of the people."

> "This is the forest primeval. The murmuring pines and the hemlocks,
> Bearded with moss and in garlands green, indistinct in the twilight,
> Stand like Druids of eld, with voices sad and prophetic,
> Stand like harpers hoar, with beards that rest on their bosoms."

In dedicating so much of the public lands to a purpose which will not be at all directly productive of revenue, the Ontario Provincial Government has done an act of far-seeing patriotism. In deciding to make a continuous and sufficient expenditure to maintain its natural features and to protect its animal life, they have recognized the fact that the people must have a grand summer playground, where they may shake off the dust and grime of the cities, and rest their weary brains amid scenes of pristine beauty.

Already the protection afforded to wild animals has been rewarded. After two years and a half had elapsed from the setting apart of the Park the superintendent reported that when he entered upon his duties scarcely a beaver could be seen, and it required close inspection to discover the presence of these animals. Already they were aware of at least sixty places in the Park where families of beaver had located themselves, in a number of cases on waters where there were no previous indications of their existence.

Among the most thrilling experiences of Canadian hunters of big game are their dangerous encounters with enraged bull moose. The fierceness must be largely confined to the sterner sex, or else the immunity from slaughter has softened the disposition of the moose in the Algonquin Park, as the following story of the Head Ranger, given in his official report, will show: "On one occasion last summer I was paddling down stream with one or two of the rangers when we unexpectedly came upon a moose cow with two calves in the water. The mother plunged out upon the bank, followed, but more leisurely, by the young ones. We landed, and had little difficulty in approaching the calves, who exhibited few signs of fear. We petted and rubbed them and offered them some pieces of bread, which they at first refused but afterwards ate with relish. All this time the cow stood some distance away, endeavouring to the utmost of her ability to attract the attention of her offspring, but to no purpose as the latter seemed to be fascinated by their newly-found friends. Even when we took to our canoes and paddled away, the young moose were unwilling to be parted from us, and ran in our wake for some time along the bank of the stream."

While travelling through the Park in winter the rangers are frequently shadowed by a single wolf who is rarely seen, and his presence is only detected by the footprints he leaves in the snow. The protection given to the deer has attracted many more wolves to the Park, and the rangers have opened active war upon them

CHAPTER XIII.

LITERATURE OF THE CAPITAL.

Royal Society of Canada—Its Objects—Various Sections—Transactions published—Its value—Other Societies—Constitutional law—Todd—Bourinot—Historians and Biographers—Scientific papers—General literature—Poetry.

Ottawa is the headquarters of the Royal Society of Canada, founded in 1882 by the Marquis of Lorne when Governor-General. Its object is the promotion of literature and science within the Dominion. It is divided into four sections, with twenty members in each; the first members were nominated by the Marquis of Lorne, and as vacancies occur they may be filled by election. The division of work among the sections is as follows :—

Sec. 1. French literature, history, archæology, etc.

Sec. 2. English literature, history, archæology, etc.

Sec. 3. Mathematics, physical and chemical sciences.

Sec. 4. Geological and biological sciences.

The general annual meeting is usually held at Ottawa in the month of May, and a large number of highly interesting and valuable papers are read in each section. They are written by members, or by others, and presented by members. A substantial vote, given by the Dominion Government, enables the Society to publish a large volume of " Transactions " annually, which contains the papers read during the year. The success of the Society is largely due to the exertions of the Honorary Secretary, Dr. J. G. Bourinot, C.M.G.

It is not to be expected that all the men of literary and scientific reputations in Canada are Fellows of the Royal Society, nor is the standing of a Fellow always accepted as being above that of his rivals who are left out. The same may be said even of the French Academy, but, on the whole, the Canadian Royal Society is doing a good work in an unostentatious way, and comprises a distinguished body of men.

There are in Ottawa, perhaps, more than the usual number of literary and scientific societies for a city of its size, say sixty-five thousand people. The comparative leisure which employment in the Civil Service gives, and the excellence of the Parliamentary Library produce this result. There are some literary and scientific societies and clubs exclusively French.

It is curious to note the trend of the writings of the Ottawa authors. Many of them have reputations wherever the English language is read. The problems of government which have been worked out in Canada during the past sixty years, have led to profound studies of the system of Parliamentary Government by Todd and Bourinot. Their works on constitutional law, history and parliamentary procedure, are the recognized authorities on those subjects.

It is natural, too, that the rich material in

Canadian archives, which Parkman treated with such marvellous skill, should be exploited by Ottawa writers. We find Mr. Sulte, Mr. DeCelles, L'Abbé Tanguay, Mr. Justice Girouard and the late Senator Tassé, among the French, and Dr. Bourinot, Dr. Kingsford, Mr. Morgan and Mr. Joseph Pope, all engaged in valuable historical or biographical work. There are many able and instructive scientific papers among the reports which get into the Blue Books, and the Director of the Geological Survey, Dr. G. M. Dawson, C.M.G., has a world-wide name not only for his able researches in geology, but for his valuable papers on the Canadian Indians.

In their contributions to general literature, through the medium of magazines and periodicals, Dr. Bourinot, Mr. M. J. Griffin, Mr. Le Sueur and the late Alphonse Lusignan and Joseph Marmette are, or were, the most prominent of Ottawa writers.

There is one branch of English literature, however, in which the Canadian capital will not yield the palm to any other city, with the exception of London, and perhaps New York. There must be something in the genesis of our nationality from a string of scattered provinces, which has thrilled its sons with new patriotic emotions, and has awakened in them the poetry that is so often poured out in a fresh flood when a nation is young.

It is remarkable that there are to-day in the Civil Service at Ottawa three young men whose true poetry has caught the ear of the literary world. It is impossible to pick up the leading magazines of England or America without finding contributions in them from William Wilfred Campbell, Archibald Lampman or Duncan Campbell Scott. They have each published volumes of their poetry, and the best literary critics are those who have praised them most highly. An apology is not necessary for giving a separate chapter to their work, and some characteristic extracts from their poetry.

CHAPTER XIV.

SOME OTTAWA POETS.

The Poetry of Archibald Lampman, William Wilfred Campbell and Duncan Campbell Scott, and a Canadian National Song.

It is not the writer's intention to enter into the vexed and fruitless question as to whether Canada possesses a poetry of her own, though perhaps the most convincing answer one could give to the random query would be an investigation of the claims of the above-named Ottawa writers to consideration among their poetical contemporaries. In the present eclipse of English poetry, when no single English writer may be said to possess a continental reputation, such a comparative investigation would lead us to the conclusion that while we need make no pretentious claims for our native writers, and though re-

LIBRARY OF PARLIAMENT, OTTAWA.

stricting them as rigidly as you will to the serried ranks of minor poets, they nevertheless have produced much admirable poetry so rooted in our soil, and so penetrated by the charm of our Canadian fields and forests, as to be impossible of growth in other lands. For this alone they deserve their appropriate praise ; but further, we are as Canadians not unsupported in the opinion that Mr. Campbell in the lyrical intensity of "The Mother," and Mr. Lampman in the exquisite realism of his landscape work, have broadened into a certain universality that transcends all purely local limitations. It will be wise, however, to restrain our steps from the thorny fields of comparative criticism, and seek to gain some characteristic insight into the more striking features of the poetry we are considering.

In discussing the work of a minor poet, we invariably ask ourselves the somewhat blunt question at the outset : Has this man an individual manner of his own, has he a characteristic and fairly novel philosophy of life, or is he at best but a diminished echo of some greater before him, and one whose highest philosophy is a bewilderment at his own small woes? In the former instance only, can criticism bear any result; so though we may suspect and even observe that Mr. Lampman is imbued with the philosophy of Wordsworth and the spirit of his poetry, we count it only as a gain. For truly it may be said, that even if his poetic message be of great necessity more slender than his master's, he has still brought to his task all that same fineness of vision, the swift correspondence of eye and brain, and above all more than a pupil's share of that sense of a brooding mystery that folds its wings over the beauties of the earth.

Even when ceasing to regard the larger limits of Mr. Lampman's work and passing into detail, one might wander through his poetry and cull richly from the ripely-rounded phrases that have matured in the sun-soaked summer fields—phrases, moreover, that linger in one's memory less perhaps for their perfect music, than because the writer's eye had lingered caressingly upon the object he describes, until the heart of its beauty was revealed. A quotation from the closing stanzas of a remarkable poem, "The Comfort of the Fields," will give some indication of his range of colour, which is quite Tennysonian in character, and will bear silent witness to the poet's intense feeling for the sounds and sights of the outer world :

In upland pastures, sown with gold, and sweet
    With the keen perfume of the ripening grass,
    Where wings of birds and filmy shadows pass,
Spread thick as stars with shining marguerite ;
To haunt old fences overgrown with brier,
    Muffled in vines, and hawthorns, and wild cherries,
    Rank poisonous ivies, red-bunched elderberries,
And pièd blossoms to the heart's desire,
    Gray mullein towering into yellow bloom,
    Pink-tasseled milkweed, breathing dense perfume,
And swarthy vervain, tipped with violet fire.

To hear at eve the bleating of far flocks,
    The mud-hen's whistle from the marsh at morn ;
    To skirt with deafened ears and brain o'erborne

Some foam-filled rapid charging down its rocks
With iron roar of waters; far away
    Across wide-reeded meres, pensive with noon,
    To hear the querulous outcry of the loon ;
To lie among deep rocks, and watch all day
    On liquid heights the snowy clouds melt by ;
Or hear from wood-capped mountain-brows the jay
    Pierce the bright morning with his jibing cry.

To feast on summer sounds ; the jolted wains,
    The thrasher humming from the farm near by,
    The prattling cricket's intermittent cry,
The locust's rattle from the sultry lanes ;
Or in the shadow of some oaken spray,
    To watch, as through a mist of light and dreams,
    The far-off hay-fields, where the dusty teams
Drive round and round the lessening squares of hay,
    And hear upon the wind, now loud, now low,
With drowsy cadence half a summer's day,
    The clatter of the reapers come and go.

Far violet hills, horizons filmed with showers,
    The murmur of cool streams, the forest's gloom,
    The voices of the breathing grass, the hum
Of ancient gardens overbanked with flowers :
Thus, with a smile as golden as the dawn,
    And cool fair fingers radiantly divine,
    The mighty mother brings us in her hand,
For all tired eyes and foreheads pinched and wan,
Her restful cup, her beaker of bright wine :
    Drink, and be filled, and ye shall understand !

Pure bits of unaffected realism abound in Mr. Lampman's maturer work. Mr. Howells drew the attention of American readers to the early poem "Heat," which is given in full below. From his later book, several poems could be named of similar inspiration and almost finer art:—"The Meadow," "June," "September," "At the Ferry," and the poem already referred to, "The Comfort of the Fields," which after all contains the substance of Mr. Lampman's philosophy. This utter dependence on Nature may often imply a tacit admission of powerlessness to cope with human problems, but with Mr. Lampman it is not so. He loves Nature not as a baffled refugee from life, but because her companionship gives him sunnier days, and sweeter life beneath the sun. Moreover, his earlier book has nothing of the enforced sameness which a book must have that bears the title "Lyrics of Earth," and there, in such a poem as "Between the Rapids," as if to vindicate his variety, is found a spirit of pensive human reverie worthy of that master of pathetic memories, Lamartine.

HEAT.

By Archibald Lampman

From plains that reel to southward, dim,
    The road runs by me white and bare;
Up the steep hill it seems to swim
    Beyond, and melt into the glare.
Upward half way, or it may be
    Nearer the summit, slowly steals
A hay-cart, moving dustily
    With idly clacking wheels.

By his cart's side the wagoner
    Is slouching slowly at his ease,
Half-hidden in the windless blur
    Of white dust puffing to his knees.
This wagon on the height above,
    From sky to sky on either hand,
Is the sole thing that seems to move
    In all the heat-held land.

Beyond me in the fields the sun
    Soaks in the grass and hath his will;
I count the marguerites one by one;
    Even the buttercups are still.

LAMPMAN'S "HEAT."

On the brook yonder, not a breath
    Disturbs the spider or the midge,
The water-bugs draw close beneath
    The cool gloom of the bridge.

Where the far elm-tree shadows flood
    Dark patches in the burning grass,
The cows, each with her peaceful cud,
    Lie waiting for the heat to pass.
From somewhere on the slope near by
    Into the pale depth of the noon
A wandering thrush slides leisurely
    His thin revolving tune.

In intervals of dreams I hear
    The cricket from the droughty ground ;
The grass-hoppers spin into mine ear
    A small innumerable sound.
I lift mine eyes sometimes to gaze ;
    The burning sky-line blinds my sight ;
The woods far off are blue with haze,
    The hills are drenched in light.

And yet to me not this or that
    Is always sharp or always sweet ;
In the sloped shadow of my hat
    I lean at rest, and drain the heat ;
Nay more, I think some blessèd power
    Hath brought me wandering idly here :
In the full furnace of this hour
    My thoughts grow keen and clear.

Turning now to Mr. Campbell's poetry, it will be at once perceived that he is much more conscious than Mr. Lampman of the hostile impact of Fate upon our life, and hence the occasional note of querulous defiance amid his music. We miss what Mr. Lampman's poetry abounds in, that spirit of gentle acquiescence in the scheme of things, with its occasional vague wonder at the mysteries that enfold our life, and give to the Earth's beauties their keener edge of rapture. Yet what we miss of philosophic calm, we gain in lyrical passion, and the mood which Mr. Campbell works in should, as his mind and art ripen with the years, be more fertile in powerful work, tinged though it might be, or perhaps because tinged with the sombre hues of pessimism.

Of a truth, when we seek to exemplify the nature of this pessimism from his accomplished work we are almost baffled, for it is rather in its subtler tendencies that we perceive the pessimistic bias. There are verses, however, that burn with a fierce fire of protest against the World's blind indifference to human worth, and of these "Pan the Fallen," with the strong pathos of its symbolism, is the most artistic. (This poem is also given in full below.) Of the same tendency also are his numerous poems infused with a weird and subtle mysticism that seems born of a fusion of Coleridge and of Poe. Or again we might instance his predilection for situations that depict the bewildered, inalienable despair of some weak nature shuddering with the taint of an awful crime upon it. It is impossible therefore to escape the influence of that pervading sombre mood in the poetry of Mr. Campbell, and even in the domain of Nature he seeks less often to elude than to satisfy those gloomy affinities of his soul.

Thus, by the compelling exigencies of their varied natures, a prevailing tone dominates the poetry alike of Mr. Campbell and of Mr. Lampman. Mr. Campbell's early book,

"Lake Lyrics," is almost monotonously burdened by the splendid desolation that broods, with its own peculiar charm, between shore and sky-line in our northern lakes, and Mr. Lampman's later book revels, with an equally pardonable repetition, in the fulness of inland beauties; yet after all, this fascination to which both are subject reveals less, perhaps, the limitation of their powers, than their ardent susceptibility to the various beautiful aspects of Nature, which they adequately and lovingly reproduce.

Disregarding the many excellent Swinburnian rhythms of Mr. Campbell's earlier work, with their Swinburnian glamour of musical landscape, it is only fair to make a few selections of a different character than indicated above, which will show also his skill in striking out flashes of fine poetry within the compass of a verse or line. Though yielding the palm to Mr. Lampman for local fidelity in description, the following verses would lead one to desire and to expect others of a kindred exact and picturesque character. The quotation is from the body of the poem "An August Reverie."

> The ragged daisy starring all the fields,
>   The buttercup abrim with pallid gold,
> The thistle and burr-flowers hedged with prickly shields,
>   All common weeds the draggled pastures hold,
> With shrivelled pods and leaves are kin to me,
> Like heirs of earth and her maturity.
>
> They speak in silent speech that is their own,
>   These wise and gentle teachers of the grass;
> And when their brief and common days are flown,
>   A certain beauty from the year doth pass—
> A beauty of whose light no eye can tell,
> Save that it went; and my heart knew it well.

It is a bold thing to enter into the dangerous rivalry which an Ode to Autumn entails, when Keats and Watson have essayed to sing her praises. The exquisite picture which the following three lines contain is in itself a sufficient justification for the attempt.

> Maiden of veilèd eyes and sunny mouth,
> Dreaming between hushed heat and frosted lands;
> With fire-mists in thine eyes, and red leaves in thy hands.

It has not been the writer's wish to contrast these two poets to the advantage of either. They are both men of strong and independent intellects, and have done admirable work in their separate fields. A beautiful landscape yields a richer harvest of thought to Mr. Lampman's imagination, but then, as if in compensation, he lacks that feeling for the remoter mystical aspects of life which produced the remarkable poem of "The Mother," with its strange and forcible appeal from the realm of weird and unhealthy fancies to the common and healthy instincts of the human heart. There is no space here to discuss Mr. Campbell's dramatic work, which adequately fulfills the promise of his other poetry; and the narrative verse of each poet might also be dismissed with the moderate words of praise their excellence demands.

PAN THE FALLEN.
By William Wilfred Campbell.

He wandered into the market
    With pipes and goatish hoof;

He wandered in a grotesque shape,
    And no one stood aloof.
For the children crowded round him,
    The wives and greybeards too,
To crack their jokes and have their mirth,
    And see what Pan would do.

The Pan he was they knew him,
    Part man, but mostly beast,
Who drank, and lied, and snatched what bones
    Men threw him from their feast;
Who seemed in sin so merry,
    So careless in his woe,
That men despised, scarce pitied him,
    And still would have it so.

He swelled his pipes and thrilled them,
    And drew the silent tear;
He made the gravest clack with mirth
    By his sardonic leer.
He blew his pipes full sweetly
    At their amused demands,
And caught the scornful, earth-flung pence
    That fell from careless hands.

He saw the mob's derision,
    And took it kindly, too,
And when an epithet was flung,
    A coarser back he threw;
But under all the masking
    Of a brute, unseemly part,
I looked, and saw a wounded soul,
    And a god-like, breaking heart.

And back of the elfin music,
    The burlesque, clownish play,
I knew a wail that the weird pipes made,
    A look that was far away—
A gaze into some far heaven
    Whence a soul had fallen down;
But the mob only saw the grotesque beast
    And the antics of a clown.

For scant-flung pence he paid them
    With mirth and elfin play,
Till, tired for a time of his antics queer,
    They passed and went their way;
Then there in the empty market
    He ate his scanty crust,
And, tired face turned to heaven, down
    He laid him in the dust.

And over his wild, strange features
    A softer light there fell,
And on his worn, earth-driven heart
    A peace ineffable.
And the moon rose over the market,
    But Pan, the beast, was dead;
While Pan, the god, lay silent there,
    With his strange, distorted head.

And the people, when they found him,
    Stood still with awesome fear.
No more they saw the beast's rude hoof,
    The furtive, clownish leer;

> But the lightest in that audience
>   Went silent from the place,
> For they knew the look of a god released
>   That shone from his dead face.

This outline would not be complete without a reference to the poetry of Mr. Duncan Campbell Scott. It has few points of actual contact with the poetry that has been discussed, and is much more dependent for its effect upon the artistic character of the workmanship, which often, it must be confessed, leaves the human interest somewhat attenuated. "The Magic House" and "The Reed Player" are the most artistically satisfying poems in the collection, and show the author keenly alive to the subtle vanishings and mystical visitations that baffle or beset our mortality. The verses "In the Country Churchyard" have a stately and appropriate beauty sustained and strengthened by the quiet dignity of the thought. The poem closes in a serene glow of colour that relieves the whole from any possible sombreness of effect.

> Rest here, for day is hot to follow you,
>   Rest here until the morning star has come,
>   Until is risen aloft dawn's rosy dome,
> Based deep on buried crimson into blue,
>   And morn's desire
> Has made the fragile cobweb drenched with dew
>   A net of opals veiled with dreamy fire.

This slight sketch of Mr. Scott's verse cannot be more appropriately closed than by a poem of his, which, apart from its dramatic excellence, is thoroughly and characteristically Canadian.

AT THE CEDARS.
By Duncan Campbell Scott.

> You had two girls—Baptiste—
> One is Virginie—
> Hold hard—Baptiste !
> Listen to me.
>
> The whole drive was jammed
> In that bend at the Cedars,
> The rapids were dammed
> With the logs tight rammed
> And crammed ; you might know
> The Devil had clinched them below.
>
> We worked three days—not a budge,
> " She's as tight as a wedge, on the ledge,"

Says our foreman:
"Mon Dieu! boys, look here,
We must get this thing clear."
He cursed at the men
And we went for it then;
With our cant-dogs arow,
We just gave he-yo-ho;
When she gave a big shove
From above.

The gang yelled and tore
For the shore;
The logs gave a grind
Like a wolf's jaws behind,
And as quick as a flash,
With a shove and a crash,
They were down in a mash,
But I and ten more,
All but Isaac Dufour,
Were ashore.

He leaped on a log in the front of the rush,
And shot out from the bind
While the jam roared behind;
As he floated along
He balanced his pole
And tossed us a song.
But just as we cheered,
Up darted a log from the bottom,
Leaped thirty feet square and fair,
And came down on his own.

He went up like a block
With the shock,
And when he was there
In the air,
Kissed his hand
To the land;
When he dropped
My heart stopped,
For the first logs had caught him
And crushed him;
When he rose in his place
There was blood on his face.

There were some girls, Baptiste,
Picking berries on the hillside,
Where the river curls, Baptiste,
You know—on the still side.
One was down by the water;
She saw Isaac
Fall back.

She did not scream, Baptiste,
She launched her canoe;
It did seem, Baptiste,
That she wanted to die too,
For before you could think,
The birch cracked like a shell
In that rush of hell,
And I saw them both sink.

Baptiste!
He had two girls,

> One is Virginie,
> What God calls the other
> Is not known to me.

A CANADIAN NATIONAL SONG.

Many years ago public competition was invited, and a prize was awarded, for the best Canadian National Song. The writer of these sketches had the good fortune to win the prize. His lyric was set to music, and, to a limited extent, it has been sung or recited ever since throughout the Dominion; although its music has been by no means adopted as the National Air. It was one of the outbursts of nascent Canadian patriotism stimulated among our youth by the Federation of the Provinces, and the creation of the Dominion. As a specimen of that class of literary work it is given here.

THIS CANADA OF OURS.
A National Song. By J. D. EDGAR.

> Let other tongues in older lands
>   Loud vaunt their claims to glory,
> And chaunt in triumph of the past,
>   Content to live in story.

Tho' boasting no baronial halls,
    Nor ivy-crested towers,
What past can match thy glorious youth,
    Fair Canada of ours?
        Fair Canada,
        Dear Canada,
    This Canada of ours.

We love those far-off ocean Isles,
    Where Britain's monarch reigns;
We'll ne'er forget the good old blood
    That courses through our veins;
Proud Scotia's fame, old Erin's name,
    And haughty Albion's powers,
Reflect their matchless lustre on
    This Canada of ours.
        Fair Canada,
        Dear Canada,
    This Canada of ours.

May our Dominion flourish then,
    A goodly land and free,
Where Celt and Saxon, hand in hand,
    Hold sway from sea to sea;
Strong arms shall guard our cherished homes,
    When darkest danger lowers,
And with our life-blood we'll defend
    This Canada of ours.
        Fair Canada,
        Dear Canada,
    This Canada of ours.

Houses of Parliament Front View.

CHAPTER XV.

LEADING EVENTS FROM 1861 TO 1898.

Lord Monck—Deadlocks and political difficulties preceding Confederation—Cartier-Macdonald Ministry—J. Sandfield Macdonald—Sicotte—Dorion—Elections—Resignation of J. S. Macdonald—Failures to form ministry—Taché-Macdonald Ministry—Its Defeat—Political paralysis—George Brown proposes a Federal Union—Coalition formed for that purpose—Charlottetown and Quebec Conferences—Confederation—Lord Lisgar—Hudson's Bay claims extinguished—Half-breed rising—Col. (Lord) Wolseley suppresses it—British Columbia enters Confederation—The Earl of Dufferin—Prince Edward Island joins Dominion—Fall of Sir John Macdonald's Ministry—Alexander Mackenzie's Ministry—Its defeat at the Polls on the question of Protection—Lord Dufferin's popularity—Marquis of Lorne—Protective Tariff—The Princess Louise—Royal Society founded—Marquis of Lansdowne—Half-breed rebellion—Completion of Canadian Pacific—The Earl of Derby—Death of Sir John Macdonald—Sir John Abbott becomes Premier—His death—Succeeded by Sir John Thompson—The Earl of Aberdeen—The Earl and Countess old friends in Canada—Death of Sir John Thompson—Sir Mackenzie Bowell becomes Premier—His resignation—Sir Charles Tupper forms a Government—Mr. Wilfrid Laurier becomes Prime Minister.

To take in at a glance the events which have directly led up to the present position of Canada, as a self-governing commonwealth, is the object of this chapter, and it is only necessary, for that purpose, to go back to 1861. In that year Lord Monck became Governor General, and witnessed the deadlock and political paralysis, arising from the growing divergence of interests between Upper and Lower Canada, which had been united in a Legislative Union for twenty years. In this chapter is given a brief sketch of the different administrations, and leading events, during the terms of each Governor from Lord Monck to Lord Aberdeen.

LORD MONCK, 1861-8.

This Governor witnessed the "deadlock" in the Canadian Parliament, and the Quebec Conference, when the basis of Confederation was laid. He assisted the Canadian delegates at the London Conference with the Imperial Ministers in arranging the terms of the British North America Act, of 1867. His term was extended that he might see the consummation of years of work and anxiety, and in Her Majesty's name he was permitted to proclaim his appointment on 1st of July, 1867, as the Governor General of the new Dominion.

Under Lord Monck there were several Premiers, several sets of advisers, and repeated difficulties in the formation of administrations. Upon his arrival in Canada he found the Cartier-Macdonald Ministry in power, with Mr. G. E. (afterwards Sir George) Cartier as Premier, and Mr. John A. (afterwards Sir John) Macdonald as Upper Canada leader. This government fell in May, 1862, upon their Militia Bill, and Mr. J. Sandfield Macdonald became First Minister with Mr. L. V. Sicotte as Lower Canada leader. This administration suffered defeat in the House and Mr. J. Sandfield Macdonald appealed to the country in June, 1863, but not until he had very completely reconstructed his Cabinet with Hon. A. A. (afterwards Sir Antoine) Dorion as Lower Canada leader. The new House was very closely divided, though the Ministry worried through their first session held in the Autumn of 1863, but when the Parliament met again in February, 1864, it became apparent that Mr. J. S. Macdonald had no working majority, and on the 21st of March, his government voluntarily resigned.

Public affairs had become most critical. The two Provinces seemed hopelessly divided. Lord Monck appealed first to Mr. Ferguson-Blair, the ex-Provincial Secretary of the last administration, who made the attempt to form a cabinet but failed. Mr. Cartier next tried and failed. At last Sir Etienne Taché was able to get a cabinet together with Mr. John A. Macdonald as Upper Canada leader. After recess the new ministers met the House on the 3rd of May, and suffered defeat by a majority of two on the 14th of June. The great crisis had arrived and a complete "deadlock" paralyzed the system of government adopted for United

Canada in 1841. The leaders of the two parties, Mr. John A. Macdonald and Mr. George Brown, struck hands and agreed that there must be a Federal Union of the two Canadas, as the Legislative Union had broken down. A coalition government was formed for this special purpose under Sir Etienne Taché. By a fortunate coincidence, the Maritime Provinces of Nova Scotia, New Brunswick and Prince Edward Island had arranged for a conference to discuss a Federal Union among themselves at Charlottetown, P.E.I. This was taken advantage of to consider the grand scheme of a union of all the Provinces. Hence came about the Quebec Conference in 1864, Confederation and the Dominion of Canada in 1867. Sir John Macdonald was the first Premier of the Dominion.

LORD LISGAR, (SIR JOHN YOUNG), 1868-72.

During his regime, the Hudson's Bay Company's claims in the North-west were bought out by Canada. The rising among the Half-Breeds there took place with its tragic incident of the shooting of Thomas Scott. Colonel (now Lord) Wolseley, led an expeditionary force to Fort Garry with that same consummate skill, vigour, and dash, which have placed him at the head of the armies of Britain. The rebellion collapsed and Manitoba became a province of Canada, as did the Pacific Colony of British Columbia.

THE EARL OF DUFFERIN, 1872-8.

Prince Edward Island joined Confederation in his first year of office. In 1873, the Ministry of Sir John Macdonald fell, and a Liberal administration, under Mr. Alexander Mackenzie held office for five years. Sir John Macdonald then carried the country on a policy of Protection to native industries, and on the 10th of October, 1878, the Governor General installed his former Premier in that high office which he held during the rest of his life. A week afterwards, Lord Dufferin sailed from the shores of Canada, and no representative of the Crown had ever won so large a measure of popularity.

MARQUIS OF LORNE, 1878-83.

In 1879, the Canadian customs tariff was raised beyond the requirements of revenue and with the avowed object of protection to native industries. This continued to be the financial policy of the Dominion, and was approved at general elections held in 1882, 1887 and 1891. The people, at last, in the general elections of 1896, declared in favour of a modification of the protective features of the tariff. The occupancy of Government House by the Princess Louise during her husband's term of office, was generally accepted by Canadians as a friendly and sensible step, which indicated the existence of a feeling at the very heart of the Empire of more than ordinary interest in us.

The Royal Society was founded by Lord Lorne.

MARQUIS OF LANSDOWNE, 1883-8.

The second rebellion of the Half-breeds took place in the North-West Territories, and was suppressed by the Canadian Militia, after some bloodshed, in 1885. In the same year the Canadian Pacific Railway was completed across the continent. No Ministerial crisis disturbed the political atmosphere under Lord Lansdowne, and he was not often called upon to exercise before the public eye the marked abilities, and the ripe knowledge of affairs, which he has since shown in the service of the Empire.

THE EARL OF DERBY, (LORD STANLEY OF PRESTON), 1888-93.

The death of Sir John Macdonald occurred in 1891, and the leader of his government in the Senate, Sir John Abbott, became Premier. The latter died in 1892, and Sir John Thompson, Minister of Justice, and Conservative leader in the House of Commons, formed a government as First Minister. In Lord Derby Canada had a Governor, whose experience in Imperial administrations had made it easy for him to be a perfectly safe constitutional ruler, and whose invariable tact on all occasions rendered him a popular representative of Her Majesty.

THE EARL OF ABERDEEN, 1893.

Neither His Excellency nor the Countess of Aberdeen were strangers to Canada in 1893, as they had already spent a winter in Hamilton, and had resided on their large ranch in British Columbia. They were, therefore, warmly received as old friends. In December, 1894, Sir John Thompson died suddenly at Windsor Castle, immediately after the ceremony of being sworn in as Imperial Privy Councillor. One of his colleagues, Sir Mackenzie Bowell, the leader in the Senate, was called in by Lord Aberdeen, and succeeded in forming a government composed of the same members as before the change of Premiers. The decision of this government to introduce federal legislation to force separate Roman Catholic schools upon the Province of Manitoba against the will of the Provincial Legislature, caused much political disturbance, and produced several ministerial crises. To restore even outward harmony among his turbulent advisers was no easy task for Lord Aberdeen. A notable change was the introduction into the Bowell Cabinet of Sir Charles Tupper, Bart., who had thrown up the Canadian High Commissionership in England. He at once secured a seat, and was chosen as leader of the Government in the House of Commons.

The seventh Parliament of Canada expired by effluxion of time on the 23rd of April, 1896, terminating with the sixth session held in its life of five years. On the 27th of April, Sir Mackenzie Bowell resigned, and Sir Charles Tupper, having been called in as Premier, formed an administration and appealed to the country. At the general elections held on the

THE LAURIER ADMINISTRATION. 189

23rd of June, the Government sustained a defeat, Sir Charles Tupper resigned on the 8th of July, and the leader of the Liberal Opposition, Hon. Wilfrid Laurier, member for Quebec East, was called upon to form an administration, which he succeeded in doing.

The course of Lord Aberdeen in connection with the change of Government after the general elections has been criticised by some of the unsuccessful party. The question involved is of a controversial nature, and it does not come within the scope of this brief chronicle to discuss its merits. Lord Aberdeen's action, however, received the approval of the Canadian House of Commons and of the Imperial Government.

CHAPTER XVI.

THE FUTURE OF CANADA.

Canada a North American Community——Destiny to be worked out on this Continent——Our Neighbours——Part of a European Empire——Subjects of Queen of Canada——She gives free play to our Democratic Government——No early agitation for change probable——Area and population compared with other independent countries in Europe and America——Canada as ally of England ——French Population of Quebec no Obstacle to National unity—— Example of Switzerland——Ten generations of French Canadians ——No other land for their love——Wise treatment by England—— Their loyalty to Canada——De Salaberry——Annexation not a live Question——Commercial coercion of Canada useless——Forcible Annexation equally useless——Treaty of Arbitration between England and the United States——Jingo Opposition to it——Contribution to Imperial Defences.

What destiny does the future enfold for Canada? Though acknowledging a European allegiance, and bound by many ties of blood, and love, and interest, to England, we are essentially a North American community. Canadians propose to live here, and not to migrate to any other continent or hemisphere. Actually and potentially we are North Americans. Whatever our national destiny may be, it must be worked out, in its internal or domestic features, on a portion of the earth's surface which extends from the Atlantic to the Pacific along the Northern boundary of the United States for over three thousand miles. These are our physical conditions, to which we are bound as is the tortoise to his shell. If we were disposed to be quarrelsome, our agressions could only reach the Yankee or the Eskimo.

We find ourselves, however, enjoying practical political freedom, though forming a portion of a European Empire. We use the name of the Queen as the symbol of the will of the people of Canada. We are no longer subjects of subjects, but we are subjects of the Queen of Canada, who reigns in England too. No question has arisen among Canadians of changing the constitutional head of our state, any more than it has arisen even among the

Radicals and Republicans in England. It is impossible that any elected head of the State could give freer play to our democratic forms of popular government than is given both in England and Canada to-day by a hereditary monarch. It may be safely concluded that no agitation will arise for many years to alter the present political status of Canada, unless some unlikely act of fatuous folly by the statesmen of Great Britain should threaten to impair our self-governing powers.

Canadians do not, and should not be expected to, shut their eyes to the importance of their country in all elements which make for national strength. Laying aside all consideration of our immense fertile areas, and our natural resources, rich beyond calculation, we are not inferior, even in population, to many monarchies and states of Europe. Our population exceeds that of Denmark and Greece combined; it equals that of Norway and Switzerland combined; and we are as populous as Portugal, or Sweden, or the Netherlands. In 1890, at Washington, was held a notable assemblage of the representatives of seventeen independent nations of the Western Hemisphere. They entered into a comprehensive treaty for settling most of their disputes by arbitration. Canada was not invited. Among all these nations the populations of fourteen were less than that of Canada. Apart from the United States, Canada would rank fourth as to revenue, and as to territory she would outrank them all, even Brazil. The marked isolation of Canada from her fellow nations in America is not an unmixed evil, yet it is a fact that must possess some significance.

In any event it is the part of patriotic Canadians to take stock of their national outfit, for in all but the name we are a nation now.

As an argument against the hope, which we all cherish, of a permanent and national unification of the various Canadian Provinces, it has been urged that in Quebec there is a large central population differing from the rest in race, language and religion. History teaches us that the national sentiment can obliterate these distinctions, and that when once the flame of patriotic ardour has been kindled, it has force to fuse them into a fervent love of country that can overcome the traditions of ancient strifes and warring creeds. In our time there exists in the midst of the armaments of Europe, a people whose patriotism is proverbial, and yet they combine the greatest diversities of race, language and religion. The brave little Swiss Republic comprises French, Germans and Italians, all speaking their own tongues, and worshipping in Protestant and Catholic Churches in almost equal numbers. Has anyone doubted the patriotism of the Swiss?

May it not be asked, has anyone had reason to doubt the patriotism of the French-Canadians? They have a record, and an old one, of devotion to their native land.

Before the Pilgrim Fathers landed on Plymouth Rock, and more than a hundred years before an enterprising young Canadian founded the city of New Orleans, the foundations of Quebec were laid. While the Dutch were peopling the banks of the Hudson, and when the turbulent pioneers of Virginia first began to occupy the broad lands of the old Dominion, the fair plains and proud cities of Normandy and Bretagne were sending forth their brave and hardy sons to dwell beside the waters of the mighty St. Lawrence. For ten generations son has succeeded to father in the French-Canadian parishes of Quebec. More than a century ago the fortunes of war severed them from their mother-land, but their love for her has not faded. France has changed, and no political alliance is sought by her Canadian children; but their hearts are still full of a sentimental devotion to the beautiful home of their ancestors. England, with generous wisdom, has made no distinction between her treatment of British and of French Canadians; and this policy has prevented political discontent among the Gallic race.

And what has been the result of this

peculiar position of the French in Canada? Cut off from all close political sympathies with Europe, they turn towards their native land, which they cherish with a tender affection, for what country is left for them to love if it be not Canada? And love it they do, with all the enthusiasm of which their ardent natures are capable. No other countries have, for them, such mountains or such rivers as their own. From Gaspé to Lachine old traditions linger among the people, and they glory in a French-Canadian literature of great merit. In the long winter evenings, and in the soft twilights of a northern summer, may be heard throughout the land the echoes of sweet and simple melodies; these are their *chansons,* or songs of the people—Canadian words sung to Canadian airs. The brave voyageurs had their merry boat songs for generations before Tom Moore supplied us with his.

If the *habitants* fought to the bitter end to save Canada from the British invaders of 1759, so were they to be found rallying under the standard of a De Salaberry to repulse the American invaders of their soil in 1812. The French-Canadian owns no divided allegiance. It is "Canada First" and Canada to the last, with him. There is no more hopeful element of national strength in the Dominion of Canada than the solid mass of Canadian patriotism that exists in the Province of Quebec.

The question of annexation to the United States is not a live one in Canada. Some hot-heads south of the border are always to be found advocating the forcing of Canada into the Union by hostile commercial legislation. If they would only reflect a little, and ascertain the views of Canadians on the subject, they would come to the conclusion that coercion of any kind would only have the effect of embittering our people against theirs. It is not likely that thoughtful Americans, themselves, would be too eager to receive such an enormous addition to their territory, and to their problems of government, even if Canada were to propose a political union. To speculate upon a forcible annexation of Canada is idle. Even if war should break out between Britain and the United States, and Canada were for the time overrun by the vast armies of the Republic, it would only be after a resistance so fierce and desperate as to render any sort of political amalgamation impossible.

The efforts to establish a treaty of general arbitration for all differences between Great Britain and the United States are of the deepest interest to Canadians.

The small Jingo element among us are against it. They predict that it will never pass the United States Senate, and that if it should be passed the Americans would not work it out honestly. It is curious that the Jingoes in the United States, or the Tail Twisters, seem to agree with Canadian Jingoes in opposition to the grandest step forward in international relations which has been attempted this century.

The question of Canada's sharing in Imperial Defence is a difficult problem. To protect the commerce of both countries, in case of war with a strong naval power, the sea-ports of Halifax, Quebec and Esquimalt must certainly be rendered impregnable. There should, therefore, be no difficulty in reaching a fair understanding as to apportioning the cost of those defensive works. To propose in piping times of peace to tax the people of Canada for the building of fortifications abroad, or for the support of the British army and navy, would be an unprofitable attempt. Yet no one who understands those same people of Canada can doubt that if a supreme crisis should arise in which the mother-land was threatened, the whole resources of the Dominion in men and money would be poured out in England's cause as freely as if we were a county in England herself. It would be unwise to commute to-day for any fixed contribution in money the unlimited debt of loyalty, which Canada cheerfully owes to the mother-land.

CHAPTER XVII.

CANADA AND ENGLAND.

Canada's stock-taking——A Mighty Nation's Call——What Europe thinks of England——Considers Her oppressive——An excuse given ——No Freedom on the Continent——Contrast in England——Imperial Sentiment——Canada a Democracy——Imperial Wave——. Reception of Canada at Jubilee——Foreign Treaties denounced——Cuba and Canada——Imperial Democrats——Material Prosperity not all——Fuller Responsibilities for Canada.

While Canada has been learning the lesson of standing alone, she has naturally been taking stock, as we have seen, of her own position and resources. She finds herself not poorly equipped, when compared with other nations, and possessing greater promise for the future than most of them.

Her destiny is in her own hands, but she sees a mighty nation that is beckoning her to come and share a greater future, as part of a world-wide Empire, than isolated Canada could ever hope to enjoy.

Canadians are not deaf to this call, nor have they failed to ask themselves whether England is the great, the wise and paramount power she seems to be when viewed in the glamour of their love and loyalty. What do the people of Europe think of England, and are their criticisms just?

The educated Canadian, from his political and geographical position, is more likely to form a fair idea of the estimate in which England is held by the other nations than is his somewhat insular fellow-citizen, the stay-at-home resident of the British Isles.

It is clear to Canadians that in Europe England is believed to be aggressive and grasping, as well as overbearing and oppressive, towards the weaker peoples with whom her vast territory brings her in touch.

It is probably true that the physical contact of English power with scores of uncivilized races, whose ignorance or barbarism prompted them to begin hopeless contests against her illimitable resources, has often led to the infliction of punishments that were severe. But what civilized race coming into contact with barbarism has ever been able to conduct a perfectly chivalrous and generous warfare?

Canadians can, however, recognize something to admire in the British people, that continental races have not yet achieved, and have scarcely dreamed of. Although they may at times be upheaved and torn by outbursts in the name of liberty, there is seldom continuity even in their efforts for political freedom, and personal liberty seems not yet to be understood or valued on the continent.

Apart from all questions of blood and racial antipathy, and if invited to do so, is there a first-class power in continental Europe with which Canada could coalesce to-day without political degradation? Canadians, whose political freedom and personal liberties are absolute, could not attach themselves to the destinies of any land less free than their own. If they were seeking for an ally, there is none to choose so free, so paramount in commerce, so great in literature, so full of generous and world-wide sympathies for human progress and liberty, as the great Mother of Parliaments that is calling to them from over the sea.

The Jubilee celebration of 1897, has either caused, or elicited in Canada, an Imperial sentiment, the strength of which was never before displayed or suspected. If there be a country in the world where a true democratic feeling should prevail, it is in Canada. Canadians possess a well ordered freedom that transcends the dreams of all the theorists since the days of Plato. They enjoy complete personal and religious liberty. Under their political system they govern themselves according to their own will and discretion. No aristocracy or plutocracy yet threatens to hold sway over their destiny. Wealth is equally distributed, and grim want is seldom known. Their standard of popular education is high, and their culture is developing.

If democracy be government by the people, then is Canada a pure democracy. Her citizens are wise and well-informed about the less fortunate position of many other nations, and for that reason are contented and undesirous of change. And yet this happy democracy is stirred by an Imperial wave. How has it come about, and what is the full significance of the sentiment?

The offer by Canada of certain tariff preferences to the mother-country was warmly received in the Jubilee year, as a gratifying evidence of the unity of the Empire. The Dominion Premier was a picturesque and brilliant figure, whose very nationality and frank loyalty swelled the flood of enthusiastic welcome given to all Canadian representatives. For these, and many other reasons, the popular reception accorded to Canada in England was far beyond all expectations. It flattered Canadian pride, and touched Canadian hearts.

Did they not see that a place was given them of lofty preeminence among the countless races and tongues and creeds, who bowed before the sceptre in the hands of Queen Victoria, whose name is used from day to day to symbol the majesty of law and justice in Canada?

And this whole world-wide system, of which Canadians form a part, was the Empire. Was it not true that the freest of all the nations in the Imperial circle was honoured most? Was it a little thing that, as a pledge of kinship and love, the greatest of all commercial powers denounced two of her most important commercial treaties, in order to help Canada to draw nearer to her?

Assuredly, a new epoch has at last come in the world's history, when the discovery has been made that a parent nation can bind a colony closer to her by striking off all its fetters, and can win its enduring loyalty by a gift of the broadest freedom.

It is no wonder that in looking at the new relations in which we Canadians find ourselves with the Empire, interest as well as sentiment should impel us to ponder upon the problems that surround us. Almost every foot of American soil, from Canada's border to Patagonia, has been lost by European powers, who pursued a coercive policy. Can anything better show the contrast between the old and the new colonial policies, than Canada and Cuba? If Cuba is to win her freedom it is through blood and fire and famine. Canada has had her freedom yielded to her by wise and timely concessions, and she turns towards Britain now, to see if they cannot cement the friendship between them. No radical, no democrat, no socialist reformer in Canada sees danger to the state from a closer alliance with the motherland. Our domestic liberties are not placed in jeopardy by recognizing that we are indeed a part of an Imperial system that covers the earth. Hence it is, that in Canada there are to-day many sturdy democrats with Imperialistic sympathies. Watchful as they are that not one of our precious liberties shall be impaired, and proud as they are of the Canadian name, they feel that they are also citizens of the British Empire. What obligations this will entail, and what benefits it will confer, cannot be known at present. This much we do understand, however—that no nation ever became great, no people ever emerged from Bœotian stagnation, without having the responsibility of foreign relations in some way thrust upon them.

Canada will surely be rich and powerful and prosperous, but is that enough? The virile races, whose blood courses through Canadian veins, would not wish a future for their children where a perpetual peace would reign, and the acquisition of wealth would be their chief and only aim and occupation. If the poet's fancy of a "parliament of man and a federation of the world" were to be realized, Canadians would have no desire to disturb the general harmony. It would, however, not be at all to their taste to monopolize a local millennium between their ocean bounds, while people of their kith and kin might be fighting and struggling for hearth and home in some dread battle of Armageddon.

When the day shall come, or how it is to come, we do not yet perceive, but come it must, when Canada will in some way assume a fuller share of the responsibilities of the mighty Empire, under whose protection and prestige she has grown from a feeble colony to a self-governing nation.

INDEX.

A

Abbot, Sir John, Premier of Canada, 89, 186.
Aberdeen, Countess of. Her kindly zeal and good influence, 120.
Aberdeen, Earl of. Characteristics and good influence of, 119, 120; Governor-General, 187-189.
Agriculture, Department of, 65
Algonquins—the river of, the race of, 12; on Allumette Island, 16; Pontiac, a Chief of, 25; Iroquois scattered Ottawa Tribes of, 25.
Algonquin brave killed by Iroquois, 30.
Algonquin Park—natural features of, animal life in, 148-152; area of, 148; no pot-hunting in, 149; beaver, 150, 151; moose, 151, 152; deer, wolves, 152.
Algoumequins, la rivière des, old name for the Ottawa, 12,
Alien Labor Law, 85.
Allumette Island, reached by Champlain, 16; abandoned by the Nation of the Isle, 23.
American Constitution modelled after text books, 78.
American visitors at Government house, 117.
"An August Reverie," poem by W. W. Campbell, quoted, 169.
Annexation with United States discussed, 197-8.

Arbitration Treaty, Interest of Canadians in, 198.
Architecture of Parliament Buildings, 57.
Asticou, Indian name for Chaudière Falls, 6.
Athletic Clubs, 142.
"At the Cedars," poem by D. C. Scott, quoted, 174.
Aylmer, Lord, anecdote of Philemon Wright and, 46.

B

Ball, Historical, 118.
Bass fishing near Ottawa, 142, 145, 146.
Beaver in Algonquin Park, 150, 151.
Behring Sea Question, 84.
Black Rod, Gentleman Usher of the, 95.
Bourinot. Dr. J. G., Hon. Sec'y of the Royal Canadian Society of Canada, 154; his Constitutional and Historical writings, 155, 156.
Bowell, Sir Mackenzie, Premier of Canada, 90, 187, 188.
Braddock, defeat of, 25.
Brebœuf, Jean de, Leader of Jesuit Missionaries, 21; cruel fate of, 22; skull of, a relic in Quebec, 22.
British Columbia becomes a Province of Canada, 184.
British Government decides to build the Rideau Canal, 9.
British North America Act, 68, 69, 180; division of legislative powers in, 74, 75.

210 INDEX.

Brown, Hon. George, formed coalition with Sir John A. Macdonald to accomplish Federal Union, 183.
By, Col., selects northern outlet of Rideau Canal, 9; takes up his residence on site of Ottawa, 10.
Bytown, original name of Ottawa, 10.

C

Cadieux, death song of, 26; grave of, 27, 31; awaits Iroquois at portage, 29; delays them, 29; lost in the woods, 30; sees friends, 31; lament of, 32.
Calumet, Grand Fall of, 28.
Campbell, William Wilfred, poet, 157, 166-173.
Canada, choice of Capital of, 2; United, 50; extent of, 88; future of, 190-199; a North American community, 190; compared with European nations, 192; compared with American nations, 193; attitude towards England of, 200-208; her destiny in her own hands, 200; a pure democracy, 204; stirred by an Imperial wave, 204; contrasted with Cuba, 206.
Canadian admiration for British people, 202.
Canadian Constitution compared with United States Constitution, 75, 76.
Canadian national song, 177.
Canadian Pacific Railway completed, 186.
Canoeing, 137-140.
Canoe Song of Voyageurs, 139
Capitals, national, sites of, 1.

Capital of Canada, 49-51.
Cartier, Sir George, Premier of Canada, 181.
Cartwright, Sir Richard, political career of, 108, 109; Minister of Trade and Commerce, 108; characteristics of, 109, 110; as leader of the house, 111.
Champlain, describes Chaudière Falls, 6; describes his first trip up the Ottawa, 12; sets out from St. Helen's Island and arrives at Ottawa River, 13; sees Gatineau River and Rideau Falls, 14; returns from Allumette Island, 17; describes mystic rites at Chaudière Falls, 17, 18.
Champlain ascends the Ottawa a second time, passes by Lake Nipissing and French River to Georgian Bay, visits Huron settlements, 20; leads Hurons against Iroquois, 21.
Charlottetown Conference, 183.
Chaudière Falls described by Champlain, 6; used in driving saw mills, 8; Champlain's portage at, 15; Indian rites performed at, 17, 18; Iroquois ambushes at, 24; distance from mouth of Ottawa, 37; reached by Wright's party, 42.
Chelsea Hills, a branch of Laurentian Range, 3.
Closure in British House of Commons, 92, 93; not adopted in Canada, 93.
Colonial policies, the old and the new, 206.
Commons, Canadian House of, 70-72, 83-96; Chamber of, 60-64; Bills originated by, 71;

Members of, 71, 72; Franchise of, Property Qualification abolished for, 71; Powers assigned to, 74; Controls Executive, 77, 78, 83; deals with relations between England and the United States, 85; variety of matters discussed in, 87, 88; rules of, 91, 92; sat for 129 hours, 93-94.
Constitution of Canada, 68-82.
Court, Supreme and Exchequer, 66, 67.
Cricket at Ottawa, 135.
Cuba and Canada contrasted, 206.
Curling, 128, 129.
Curtain Falls, 5.

D

Danube compared with Ottawa River, 5.
Dawson, Dr. G. M., scientific author, 156.
Deadlock in Canadian politics, 182.
DeCelles, Mr., historian, 156.
Deer-hunting, red, 147, 148.
Democratic Imperialism, 206.
Departments, Public, transferred to Ottawa, 52.
Derby, Earl of, Governor-General, 186, 187.
DeSalaberry led French Canadians against Americans, 197.
Destiny of Canada, in her own hands, 200.
DeVignan, Nicolas, sent up Ottawa River by Champlain, and returned, 12; marvellous stories of, 12; second trip up the Ottawa of, 13; convicted of falsehood by Indians and disgraced, 17.
Devil's Hole, 7.

Dickens Charles, describes Kingston, 50.
Dorion, Sir Antoine, Lower Canada leader, 181.
Drawing Room at opening of Parliament, 113-115.
Dufferin, Earl of, Governor-General, 184, 185.

E

Eastern Departmental block, officers in, 64, 65.
Elgin, Lord, attacked by Montreal mob, 51.
England, European opinion of, 201.
Exchequer Court, 66, 67.
Experimental Farms, 65, 66.
Extradition of Criminals, 84.

F

Father of the Ottawa, Philemon Wright, 36.
Fathers of Confederation, 104.
Federal Sovereignty favoured by Canadian Constitution, 75, 76.
Ferguson Blair, failed to form a cabinet, 182.
Fishing near Ottawa, 142-146; red and gray trout, 142-146; bass, 142-146; maskinonge, 146.
Follett, Miss, compares Canadian House of Commons with United States House of Representatives, 79, 80.
Football at Ottawa, 141.
Foreign Relations discussed in Canadian House of Commons, 84.
Forest Flowers, 4.
Foster, Hon. G. E., 90.

INDEX.

French Canadians, patriotism of, 196, 197.
French Members of Parliament, 72.
French River, descended by Champlain, 20.
Frontenac unable to check Iroquois, 24.

G

Game, small, near Ottawa, partridge, woodcock, wild duck, snipe, plover, 146, 147.
Gatineau River, situation of, 4; source of, 5; seen by Champlain, 14.
Georgian Bay reached by Champlain, 20.
Girouard, Mr. Justice, historian, 156.
Golf at Ottawa, 135, 136.
Gothic Architecture, supposed origin of, 58.
Government House, Ottawa, 115; winter entertainments at, 118, 119.
Governor-General, his assent to legislation required, 70; functions of, 112-120; entertainments given by, 116-119.
Grand Calumet, Falls of, 26; Island of, 27.
Grand River, old name of the Ottawa, 5, 37.
Griffin, Mr. M. J., author, 156.

H

Half-Breeds, first rebellion of, 184; second rebellion of, 186.
Head, Sir Edmund, advised Queen to select Ottawa for capital, 51.
"Heat," poem by A. Lampman, quoted, 164.

Highland Pipers of Lord Aberdeen, 116, 117.
Hockey, 127, 128.
House of Commons, see Commons, House of.
House of Representatives, Speaker of, 79, 80.
Hudson's Bay Company, bought out by Canada, 183.
Hull, City of, situation, 8; industries of, 8, 9; settlement of, 10; Philemon Wright settles on sight of, 36.
Hurons, mission to, founded by LeCaron, visited by Champlain, 20; destroyed by Iroquois, remnant go to Quebec, 22.

I

Imperial Defence, Canada's share in 198, 199.
Imperial Democrats, 206.
"In the Country Churchyard," poem by D. C. Scott, 173; quoted, 174.
Indians, their name for Chaudière Falls, 6; their superstition of the Devil's Hole, 8; their rites at Chaudière Falls, 17, 18; their attitude towards Philemon Wright, 42, 43; first to play lacrosse and use Canoes, 136, 137; see also Algonquins, Hurons, Iroquois, Ottawas, Sorcerers.
Iroquois, reasons for lying in wait at Chaudière of; canoe route to the Ottawa of, 19; burst upon St. Louis and torture Jesuit missionaries, 22; scatter tribes of Ottawa River, 22; described by Parkman, encamped at mouth of Ottawa and ravaged French

INDEX. 213

settlements, 24; Cadieux and his band surprised by, 28; held in check by Cadieux, 30.

J

Jesuit Missionaries, records of, 12; founded Huron mission, 21; abandoned Huron mission, 22.
Jingoes in Canada and the United States, 198.
Jubilee Celebration, influence on Canada of, 203-205.

K

Kingsford, Dr., historian, 156.
Kingston, Rideau Canal begins at, 9; chosen as capital by Lord Sydenham, 50.

L

"La Complainte de Cadieux," 32-34.
Lacrosse at Ottawa, 136, 137.
Lalemant, Jesuit missionary to Hurons, tortured by Iroquois, 22.
Lampman, Archibald, poet, 157-165.
Lansdowne, Marquis of, Gov.-General, 186.
LaSalle, met by Perrot on the Ottawa, 23.
Laurentian Lakes, fishing in, 142-145.
Laurentian Range, Chelsea Hills, a branch of; seen from Parliament Buildings, 56.
Laurier, Sir Wilfrid, Premier, 90, 101, 102, 103, 189; a sketch of, 99-104; personal appearance of, 99; first entrance into politics of, 100;
Minister of Inland Revenue, 101; political aims of, 103, 104.
Leader of Government, duties of, 90, 91; of Opposition, duties of, 91.
LeCaron, the first missionary among Hurons, 20.
Legend of the Ottawa, 26.
Legislatures, Provincial, 72, 73.
LeSueur, Mr., author, 156.
Library of Parliament, 57, 59, 60.
Lieut.-Governors, functions of, 73.
Lisgar, Lord, Gov.-General, 183.
Literature of the Capital, 153, 178.
London Conference, 180.
Long Sault Rapids, Iroquois ambushes at, 24; settlement extended to, 37; passed by Wright's party, 40; first raft down, 44.
Long Sessions of Canadian House of Commons, 93, 94.
Lorne, Marquis of, founded Royal Society of Canada, 153, 186; Gov.-General, 185.
Lovers' Walk near Parliament Buildings, 56.
Lusignan, Alphonse, author, 156.

M

Mace of House of Commons, 95, 96.
Major's Hill Park, 10.
Manitoba, became a Province, 184; Separate Schools of, 188.
Maple Sugar Making, 134, 135.
Marmette, Joseph, author, 156.
Maskinonge fishing near Ottawa, 146.
Michillimackinac, massacre at, 25.
Militia Bill defeated Cartier-

214 INDEX.

Macdonald Government, 181.
Monck, Lord, Gov.-General, 180-183.
Monongahala, battle of, 25.
Montreal, connected with Kingston by Rideau Canal, 9; Wright's party set out from, 39; chosen as capital of Canada; mob burns Parliament House at, 50.
Moose in Algonquin Park, 148, 151, 152.
Morgan, Mr. H. J., biographer, 156.
Macdonald, Sir John A., Upper Canada Leader, 181; formed coalition with George Brown, 183; first premier of Canada, 183; defeated, restored to power by Protection Policy, 184.
Macdonald, J. Sandfield, Premier, 181, 182.
Mackenzie, Alexander, Premier of Canada, 184.
Mackenzie Tower, 57.

N

National Capitals, choice of, 1; names of, 2.
National growth, 207.
National Song, by J. D. Edgar, 117.
Nepean Point, 10.
New France, Champlain chose Capital of, 15.
New Orleans, founded by a Canadian, 194.
New York State, home of Iroquois, 19.
Nipissing, Lake, crossed by Champlain, 20.
North, Lord, 70.
North Sea, DeVignan reports having reached, 12.

Nova Scotia, opposed to Confederation, 105.

O

Ode to Autumn, by W. W. Campbell, quoted, 169.
Ontario, Province of, bounded by Ottawa River, 8.
Ottawa City, heights of, 3; originally Bytown, changed to Ottawa in 1854, 10; beginning of political history of, 11; selected by Queen for Capital, 51.
Ottawa College Football Club, 141.
Ottawa, Father of the, Philemon Wright, 36.
Ottawa River, Capital on banks of, 2; compared to Danube, 5; at the Devil's Hole, 7; boundary between Quebec and Ontario, 8; end of Rideau Canal, 9; described by Champlain, ascended by DeVignan, 12; ascended by Champlain, 13; Philemon Wright's first exploration of, 35.
Ottawa Rowing Club, 140.
Ottawa Sports, 121, 147.
Ottawas, Indian tribe of, 12.

P

Pages of House of Commons, 63.
Pan-American Congress at Washington, 193.
"Pan the Fallen," poem by W. W. Campbell, 167; quoted, 170.
Parkman describes Iroquois on Ottawa River, 24.
Parliamentary Government adopted by Canada; never

INDEX. 215

adopted by United States, 76, 82.
Parliament sits alternately at Toronto and Quebec, 51; affirms choice of Ottawa, 52; opening and prorogueing of, 113, 114.
Parliament Buildings, site of, 3; corner stone laid, 52; site and architecture of, 54; praised by C. D. Warner, 55; arrangement of, 55, 56; kinds of stone used in, 58; rooms in, 61.
Parliament Hill, 10.
Perrot tells of meeting LaSalle, 23.
Philadelphia, delegates of 1774 at, 69.
Philemon Wright, see Wright, Philemon.
Polo at Ottawa, 135.
Pontiac, Algonquin chief, 25.
Pope, Mr. Joseph, biographer, 156.
Population of Canada, 1867, 81.
Population of United States, 1787, 81.
President's Message compared with Speech from the Throne, 78, 79.
Prince Edward Island joined Confederation, 184.
Princess Louise, 185.
Protection Policy brought Sir John Macdonald back to power, 184.
Provincial Legislatures, powers assigned to, 74, 75.

Q

Quebec City, site chosen by Champlain for Capital of New France, 15; Old Capital of Canada, 49.

Quebec Conference, 75, 180, 183.
Quebec Province, bounded by Ottawa River, 8; character of population of, 193, 197; early settlement of, 195.
Queen Victoria chose site of Capital, 2, 51.

R

Recollet priest LeCaron, first missionary among Hurons, 20.
Relations between British Empire and United States discussed by W. T. Stead, 86, 87.
Rideau Canal, origin and situation, 9; the laying out of, 47.
Rideau Falls, origin of name, 5; seen by Champlain, 14.
Rideau Hall, name for Government House, 5, 115.
Rideau Rifle Range, 147.
Rideau River supplies water for Rideau Canal, 9.
Rockcliffe, suburb of Ottawa, 140.
Royal Society of Canada, 153, 155; founded by Marquis of Lorne, 153, 186.

S

Sawmills and Factories of Hull, 8, 9.
Scott, D. C., poet, 157, 173, 177.
Scott, Thomas, shot by Halfbreeds, 184.
Second Chambers abolished in most provinces, 72, 73.
Senate Chamber of, 60; composition of, 70, 71; Premiers in, 89, 90.
Sergeant at Arms, 95.
Seven Falls, situation of, 27; portage of, 28.

Sicotte, L. V., Lower Canada Leader, 181.
Simcoe County of, seat of Huron Missions, 20.
Skating at Government House, 118, 119; in Canada, 126, 127.
Ski-lobning at Government House, 119; in Ottawa, 124, 125.
Sleigh-driving in Ottawa, 123, 124.
Snow-shoeing in Ottawa, 124, 125.
Societies, literary and scientific in Ottawa, 155.
"Song of Voyageurs," sentimental, 32; canoeing, 139, 140.
Sorcerers, an Indian tribe of Lake Nipissing, 16; visited by Champlain, 20.
Southern Departmental Block, situation, architecture, composition, 59; offices in, 65.
Sovereignty, State, favoured by United States Constitution; Federal, favoured by Canadian Constitution, 75, 76.
Sparks, Nicholas, foundation of fortune of, 47.
Speaker of United States House of Representatives, 79. 80.
Speech from the Throne compared with President's Message, 78, 79.
Stanley, Lord, see Derby, Earl of.
State Sovereignty favoured by United States Constitution, 75, 76.
Ste. Anne, a Legend of, 29.
Stead, W. T., his views of Canada's influence, 86, 87.
St. Helen's Island, Champlain sets out from, 13.
St. Lawrence, Gulf of, 4.

St. Lawrence River, 5, 9; visited by Philemon Wright, 37.
St. Louis, Huron Mission Village, assaulted by Iroquois, 22.
Sulpician priests return via Ottawa River to Quebec, 23.
Sulte, Mr., historian, 156.
Summer Sports at Ottawa, 134-152; cricket, 135; polo, 135; golf, 135, 136; tennis, 136; lacrosse, 136, 137; canoeing, 137-140; rowing, 140; football, 141; fishing 142-146; shooting, 146, 147; rifle-practice, 147; red-deer hunting, 147, 148.
Supreme Court, 66, 67.
Suspension Bridge between Ottawa and Hull, 8.
Sydenham, Lord, chose Kingston for Capital, 50.

T

Taché, Sir Etienne, Premier of Canada, 182.
Tanguay, L'Abbé, historian, 156.
Tassé, Senator, historian, 156.
Tennis at Ottawa, 136.
Terrace, view from the, 3.
"The Comfort of the Fields," poem by A. Lampman, quoted, 161.
"The Mother," poem by W. W. Campbell, 159, 170.
"This Canada of Ours," poem by J. D. Edgar, quoted, 177.
Thompson, Sir John, Premier of Canada, 186; death of, 187.
Timber of Ottawa Valley, 37; first taken to Quebec by Wright, 44.
Tobogganing at Government

INDEX.

House, 119; in Canada, 129-133.
Todd, Constitutional Writings of, 155.
Toronto, Capital of Upper Canada, 49.
Trollope, Anthony, describes Parliament Buildings, 53, 54.
Trout, red and gray, fishing, 142-146.
Tupper, Sir Charles, Premier of Canada, 90, 106, 188; Leader of Opposition, 104; Premier of Nova Scotia, 105; High Commissioner to London, 105, 106; characteristics of, 106-108; defeated in elections, 189.

U

United States, war of 1812 with, 9; influence on Canadians of Civil War of, 75; disputes with, 84.
Upper Canada, Province of, 9.

V

Victoria, Queen, chose site of capital, 2.
Vignan, Nicolas de, see DeVignan, Nicholas.
Ville Marie, a trading-post, now Montreal, 22.
Voyageurs sing Cadieux Lament, 32.

W

Wales, Prince of, lays corner stone of Parliament Buildings, 52.
Warner, C. D., praises Parliament Buildings, 55; War of 1812-14, 9.
Washington, Pan-American Congress at, 193.
Western Departmental Block, offices in, 64, 65.
Winter Entertainments at Government House, 118, 119.
Winter Furs and Robes, 123.
Winter Sports at Ottawa, 121-133; sleighdriving, 123, 124; snow-shoeing, 124, 125; ski-lobning, 124, 125; skating, 126, 127; hockey, 127, 128; curling, 128, 129; tobogganing, 129, 133.
Woburn, Home of Philemon Wright, 35.
Wolseley, Lord, led force against Half-breeds, 184.
Wolves, 148, 152.
Wright, Alonzo, Canadian M.P., 47; King of the Gatineau, 48.
Wright, Philemon, first exploration of Ottawa River by, 35; relates his story, 36; Father of the Ottawa, 36; second visit to Canada, 37; third and fourth visits to Ottawa River, 38; forms party for Canadian settlement, 39; brings settlers from Woburn to Hull, 39, 42; describes night encampment, 40; not a U. E. Loyalist, 41; success of settlement of, 44; first raft of timber to Quebec, 44; his wealth in 1824, 45; his death, 45; anecdote of Lord Aylmer and, 46.

Y

Young, Sir John, see Lisgar, Lord.

www.ingramcontent.com/pod-product-compliance
Lightning Source LLC
Chambersburg PA
CBHW032212230426
43672CB00011B/2525